It is my sincere desire that the owner of this book would find within the pages healing that only comes from our loving and caring Abba-daddy!

I speak a blessing over your life that you will come to know your Abba-daddy in the full measure of his abiding mercy and power that is available to his children.

Sincerely in His Service,

Your Sister and Your Father's Daughter

Mission of the One Heart Series

To provide milk for the babe, and strong meat for the mature. To rid all who come along on this journey of religious traditions that make us white wash graves full of dead men's bones! So, that we may say as the Apostle Paul: "OH" "That I may know him, and the power of his resurrection, and the fellowship of his sufferings, being made conformable unto his death; if by any means I might attain unto the resurrection of the dead. Not as though I had already attained, either were already perfect: but I follow after, if that I may apprehend that for which also I am apprehended of Christ Jesus. Brethren I count not myself to have apprehended: but this one thing I do, forgetting those things which are behind and reaching forth unto those things which are before, I press toward the mark for the prize of the high calling of God in Christ Jesus. Let us therefore, as many as be perfect (pure in heart, italics mine), be thus minded: and if any thing ye be otherwise minded, God shall reveal even this unto you. Nevertheless, whereto we have already attained, let us walk by the same rule, and let us mind the same thing. Brethren, be followers together of me, and mark them which walks so as ye have us for an ensample. (For many walk, of which I have told you often, and now tell you even weeping, that they are the enemies of the cross of Christ: Whose end is destruction, whose God is their belly, and whose glory is their shame, who mind earthly things.) For our conversation is in heaven; from whence also we look for the Saviour, the Lord Jesus Christ; Who shall change our vile body, that it may be fashioned like unto his glorious body, according to the working whereby he is able to even to subdue all things unto himself. (Philippians 3:10-21, KJV) our vile body, that it may be fashioned like unto his glorious body, according to the working whereby he is able to even to subdue all things unto himself.

Notice is hereby given that this author claims the full trademark rights to the all inferences of the "One", the "Heart", and the name "One Heart Series" utilized throughout the various books, tapes and any and all electronic media used to convey the One Heart Series Message.

© 2012, Patricia E. Adams
TM

Copyright © 2012 by Patricia E. Adams

Printed and bound in the United States of America. All rights reserved. No part of this book may be reproduced or transmitted in any form or by any means, electronic or mechanical, including photocopying, recording, or by an information storage and retrieval system -- except by a reviewer who may quote brief passages in a review to be printed in a magazine or newspaper -- without permission in writing from the publisher. For information please contact Shekinah Publishing House, 877/538-1363. Although the author and publisher have made every effort to ensure the accuracy and completeness of information contained in this book, we assume no responsibility for errors, inaccuracies, omissions, or any inconsistency herein. Any slights of people, places, or organizations are unintentional.

Scripture quotations are from the KING JAMES VERSION of the Bible. Printed in the United States of America
Ramsay, William M. "Galatia," International Standard Bible Encyclopaedia. Edited by James Orr. Blue Letter Bible. 1913. 5 May 2003. http://cf.blueletterbible.org/isbe/isbe.cfm?id=3638

ISBN 0-9700976-7-0
One Heart Series Devotional: Sustaining My Regained Position of Oneness & Intimacy With God for Fifty-Two Weeks
LCCN: 2010905082

ATTENTION ORGANIZATIONS, HEALING CENTERS, AND SCHOOLS OF SPIRITUAL DEVELOPMENT:
Quantity discounts are available on bulk purchases of this book for educational purposes. Special books or book excerpts can also be created to fit specific needs. For information, please contact Shekinah Publishing House, 1-877/538-1363.

Bio and Contact Information

She is a five-fold minister of the Gospel of Jesus Christ. Licensed in 1993 and Ordained in 1996, and serving her local church of The Potters House of Dallas, Texas. She is a Biblical Studies Instructor at The Potters Institute of Dallas, Texas and an author of a series of books on Inductive Bible Study.

The Series is called "One Heart" and cover how to be intimate with God. There are 5 books in this series. God has placed a strong teaching ministry within her spirit that speaks the truth in love, with a commandment to draw his people out and into an intimate relationship with their God.

God has wrought a mighty deliverance in her life from the baggage of physical, sexual, emotional, and religious bondage. Her testimony is that God is a mighty Deliverer and Restorer. Patricia is available to share her testimony of deliverance and restoration to groups across the country and around the world. Contact her for

- Revival
- Lectures
- Biblical Seminars
- Writing & Publishing Seminars
- Mass Communication Workshops
- Keynote Address
- Family Seminars (Men, Women and Children)
- Ministry of Helps
- Transitional Housing Outreach

One Heart International Ministries
Patricia E. Adams, President & Founder
Website: www.oneheartseries.com
Affiliate Program: www.oneheartseriesaffiliates.com
Radio Network: www.oneheartsoundmedianetwork.com
Email: author@oneheartseries.com

Dedication

This book is dedicated to the Many Children-

Who have been buried alive! When I say "buried alive" it is to say that Satan has so pillaged through your life to the point you feel like you should be dead. Children of all ages and stages of life, this is for you! You may seventy years old or greater but this is for the child in you that has not lived! Being a child should have its blend of joys and pains. The kinds of pains that consist of falling off a bicycle or skates; or sliding down a hill too fast! Not the kinds of pain that come from abandonment, abuse, rejection and neglectful physical, sexual and emotional atrocities done to your being! For each and every child including myself, again, I say this is for you! Abused but not DEFEATED! God has kept you alive in whatever state you are in because He has a plan for the pain inflicted in your life! We are MORE Than Conquerors through Christ Jesus! May this book bring the sustaining power of the Holy Spirit to touch you in the cracks, crevices and recesses of the brokenness of your heart and apply the healing balm of Gilead. May you find the reassurance of God's love as you study to show yourself approved to God as a workman that needeth not to be ashamed, but rightly dividing the word of truth? And that that truth would set you free! Free from the painful things you endured. Hear Jesus speak to the Lazarus in you and command you to come forth What the enemy meant for evil God will take and turn it for your good!

Acknowledgments

First and foremost I thank my "Lord and Savior" for the life experiences and revelation of the truth of His word concerning the trials that have tried me in the fire, and to the enemies of the light of the gospel of Jesus Christ! It is because of these fiery trials and those enemies that this work was accomplished.

To my son, without your understanding and support this work would not have been possible. It is a joy and pleasure being your mother. Much love to you my Precious!

And to God, who for many nights and early mornings called me into His presence and drew Rhema understanding of why so much pain and suffering had entered my life. He laid the solution before me, and asked me to apply it to the bitterness and pain of the aftershock of what had transpired in my life. For this there is no other that can take the place of Jesus Christ the Lover of My Soul!

We also wish to express special gratitude to the students who attended the initial Bible Study Training. Thank you for your faithfulness in drawing the Word of God out of my belly, and producing a river of living water within me. To Pastor Phillip P. Brown, Sr. and his Wife; Associate Pastor Ethel Brown, for their divine patience in allowing us to bring this material forth in a church bible study for 4 years.

A special appreciation to Pa-Pa and Mother Dear and Aunt Merlee for being there when needed the most. To Momma Tommie, Aunt Margie, Michele, Margie, and Junliah for coming alongside in their diverse ways.

Introduction

Foundation Scripture:
"And the very God of peace sanctify you wholly; and I pray God your whole spirit and soul and body be preserved blameless unto the coming of our Lord Jesus Christ. Faithful is he that calleth you, who also will do it." (I Thessalonians 5:23)

Jude says, Now unto him that is able to keep you from falling, and to present you faultless before the presence of his glory with exceeding joy. To the only wise God our Saviour, be glory and majesty, dominion and power, both now and ever. Amen. "What is man that though art mindful of him; the Bible records. Man is a tripartite being created in the image of God as an expression of God. The divine plan of God for his created man was that he would love Him with all of himself. This created being would have an absolute desire to fellowship with his creator; from an undivided heart.

Man was created to fulfill the purpose of God in the earth; that is to commune and glory in the benefits of God. The Word of God was the creative force that formed the heavens and the earth, and he alone holds the patent on his creation and the keys to the kingdom. Through the disobedience of one man, Adam; Satan gained legal access, permission to become the Prince of the Air, but not the Ruler of all the earth.

The Bible says that the earth is the Lords and the fullness thereof, and those that dwell within. Ownership has been Gods all alone! A song was written that said "…What Satan said was his, has been ours all alone…"

Now, Saints Jesus Christ has completed the work that his father sent him to do, and nothing else is required or shall be done. It is finished! Therefore, we should not allow Satan to continue to deceive ourselves into giving away our authority.

If you do not give him access, he can not come in!

Jesus removed Satan's rights to entangle all areas of our lives through the plan of salvation, He restored us to our original posture in God. Yet, we perish because of a lack of knowledge of the provisions of salvation. Especially, when we protect the painful wounds and fearful memories of our lives from God's healing touch. We literally allow a legal playground to be built, played on, and ruled over by Satan and his imps.

When we receive the Holy Spirit into our hearts, he brings in the entire five-fold ministry tools to run a revival in our dead spirit. The Holy Spirit empowers us to operate as God had originally planned. He lifts us from the ashes of despair!

Ashes are used to speak figuratively in the Bible to express the total destruction of a captive city. Ashes are known to be easily scattered, perishable, and, therefore, worthless. For example, when Satan held us as sinners; we were his captive cities.

But when the Power of the Word, the Blood of Jesus and the Fire of the Holy Spirit destroyed, and stripped bare the stronghold, the threat, the penalty and the sting of sin – we were made free! When something is made it is customized to fit the owner. Those strongholds can no longer rule over us, unless we allow them to!

From that landmark of despair, God becomes our Master (Adonai), Owner and Lord. Symbolizing the authority of God and the covenant relationship from the beginning of creation until the ascension of Jesus Christ. Picture an organizational chart, and the Trinity is aligned across the Top; and in a connecting line the second row links and aligns with the first row. This is what the Trinity has done; it has included those who believe with the authority to sit in heavenly places. We are heirs, co-equals with the inheritance of Jesus. Remember the Bible records that, "The Lord said unto my Lord, "Sit thou at my right hand, until I make thine enemies thy footstool." (Psalms 110:1) In Malachi 4:3, it says that to the Righteous, the wicked deeds of Satan are the "...ashes under the soles of our feet." Not that we are anything in ourselves, but Christ within us is our all. Jesus Christ, the Hope of Glory, Gods' Son and His Anointing took on himself our infirmities, and bore our sicknesses.

If you can envision the Lamb of God as He went to Calvary! Carrying the weight and burden of mans' sinful FLESH, the stinch of disease and the full penalty of sin and its consequences. There on the cross God laid upon Him the iniquities, and the wages of sin that had separated and broken our fellowship with God. Now as the children of God we partake of that sacrificial lamb, Jesus Christ. Jesus said that he would not drink again, of the cup; or eat of this bread of remembrance until he ascended into heaven.

He has ascended and destroyed the wage of sin, which was death! Hebrews 2:14, states that Satan's stronghold was destroyed and those who had been held in hell through fear of death who were all their lifetime subject to bondage were released. Through Jesus' death, burial, resurrection and ascension there is deliverance for us today! We have now been settled and grounded in Jesus Christ and His Anointing. As we are continuously filled with the Holy Spirit, enabled or rather empowered to remain steadfast and unmovable, like trees that are planted by the rivers of living water.

Reflection

"Just because someone did not or does not love you the way that you think they should, doesn't mean they don't love you with all they have."

We all know someone, or have known someone or persons who have not loved us as we hoped they would. Whether they were biological, or intimate, or you were victimized by both. They only gave you what they had, but now it is time to move past what they did not have to give us and give ourselves what we deserve! Freedom from carrying around the dead weight of the people who have left us feeling empty and neglected and move into position to receive love from one who can love us to the maximum capacity of what we have made room to receive. Spring (deliverance) is in the air friends, in the natural and the spirit, while we spring clean our houses, garages and offices, how about the clutter in our souls. Just by faith, not by feeling release those who have hurt you in the past and the present from a debt they can not pay, the check you are waiting to cash will bounce anyway, because remember they can not give you what they don't have. Be free in the matchless and marvelous name of the lover of your soul Jesus Christ!" Again, may you find restoration and wholeness on every page for your life!

Your Sister in His Service Until He Shouts!

Objective of One Heart Series Devotional

Heart (apopsucho) from the heart. Heart (kardia) the seat and center of human life. As the seat of the desires, feelings, affections, passions, impulses of the heart or mind. He pure in heart meaning those whose center of life has been made pure by Jesus Christ. Heart (ex holes tes kardias) meaning with the whole heart. A man after his won heart, meaning therefore approved and beloved. (Acts 13:22) The inner man (I Peter 3:4) The New Testament heart is the place of meeting for God to influence our lives. In the heart faith springs up, dwells, and works (Acts 15:9), and unbelief draws men away from belief in God. (Hebrews 3:2) It is also the place of haunts of unclean lusts that make men blind to the truth of God. (Romans 1:24). But God sends His spirit of his son to take up abode. This becomes the hidden life that lies open clearly to God's eyes which necessitates us having a heart that is right in the sight of God. (Acts 8:21)

The prototype of our relationship of Intimacy with God was built by Solomon according to God's specifications in II Chronicles 7:11-22: 11 Thus Solomon finished the house of the LORD, and the king's house: and all that came into Solomon's heart to make in the house of the LORD, and in his own house, he prosperously effected.

God appears to Solomon and gives him some conditional promises   12 And the LORD appeared to Solomon by night, and said unto him, I have heard thy prayer, and have chosen this place to myself for an house of sacrifice. 13 If I shut up heaven that there be no rain, or if I command the locusts to devour the land, or if I send pestilence among my people; 14 If my people, which are called by my name, shall humble themselves, and pray, and seek my face, and turn from their wicked ways; then will I hear from heaven, and will forgive their sin, and will heal their land. 15 Now mine eyes shall be open, and mine ears attent unto the prayer that is made in this place. 16 For now have I chosen and sanctified this house, that my name may be there for ever:

and mine eyes and mine heart shall be there perpetually. 17 And as for thee, if thou wilt walk before me, as David thy father walked, and do according to all that I have commanded thee, and shalt observe my statutes and my judgments; 18 Then will I stablish the throne of thy kingdom, according as I have covenanted with David thy father, saying, There shall not fail thee a man to be ruler in Israel. 19 But if ye turn away, and forsake my statutes and my commandments, which I have set before you, and shall go and serve other gods, and worship them; 20 Then will I pluck them up by the roots out of my land which I have given them; and this house, which I have sanctified for my name, will I cast out of my sight, and will make it to be a proverb and a byword among all nations. 21 And this house, which is high, shall be an astonishment to every one that passeth by it; so that he shall say, Why hath the LORD done thus unto this land, and unto this house? 22 And it shall be answered, Because they forsook the LORD God of their fathers, which brought them forth out of the land of Egypt, and laid hold on other gods, and worshipped them, and served them: therefore hath he brought all this evil upon them.

We will examine over 50 heart types in the Bible that will allow for self-examination and sustaining of your "Intimacy with God". Again, may you find restoration and wholeness on every page of this devotional for your life!

Be Thou Sustained in the Name of Jesus!

Table of Contents

Mission of the One Heart Series iii
Dedication xi
Acknowledgments xiii
Introduction xv
Reflection xix
Objective of One Heart Series Devotional xxi
Significance of Day and Time of Devotion 1
The Danger of Little Things 2
How Do We Walk in the Spirit – Surrendered 3
There Are 17 Works Of The Flesh: 16
Weekly Plan Outline: Day 1 19
   Saturday Remember Put on Your Armour! 19
Weekly Plan Outline: Day 2 20
   Sunday Remember Put on Your Armour! 20
Weekly Plan Outline: Day 3 21
   Monday Remember Put on Your Armour! 21
Weekly Plan Outline: Day 4 22
   Tuesday Remember Put on Your Armour! 22
Weekly Plan Outline: Day 5 23
   Wednesday Remember Put on Your Armour! 23
Weekly Plan Outline: Day 6 27
   Thursday Remember Put on Your Armour! 27
Weekly Plan Outline: Day 7 28
   Friday Remember Put on Your Armour! 28
What is the Heart: Holman 29
What is The Heart: Faussets 33
The Heart: Old Testament Hebrew Lexicon 34
The Renewed Heart: Torrey's Topical Textbook 35

The Unrenewed Heart: Torrey's Topical Textbook 36
Some Heart Types in the Bible 39
Some Heart Types in the Bible cont'd 40
Buried Alive 41
Buried Alive continued 42
Buried Alive conclusion 43
Touching the Taboo 45
The Pages of My Life 47
Week One: Broken Heart 55
Week Two: Heart of Wax 61
Week Three: Grieved Heart 67
Week Four: Willing Heart 73
Week Five: Faithful Heart 79
Week Six: Communing and Sound Heart 85
Week Seven: Proud Heart 91
Week Eight: Wicked Heart 97
Week Nine: Trembling Heart 103
Week Ten: Perfect Heart 109
Week Eleven: Meek Heart 115
Week Twelve: Double Heart 121
Week Thirteen: Tender Heart 127
Week Fourteen: Soft Heart 133
Week Fifteen: Pure Heart 139
Week Sixteen: Upright Heart 145
Week Seventeen: Clean Heart 151
Week Eighteen: Established Heart 157
Week Nineteen: Inditing Heart 163
Week Twenty: Honest Heart 169
Week Twenty-One: Wise Heart 175
Week Twenty-Two: Merry Heart 181
Week Twenty-Three: Sorrowful Heart 187
Week Twenty-Four: Haughty Heart 193
Week Twenty-Five: Failing Heart 199

Week Twenty-Six: Heavy Heart 205
Week Twenty-Seven: Unsearchable Heart 211
Week Twenty-Eight: Despiteful Heart 217
Week Twenty-Nine: Bitter Heart................................ 223
Week Thirty: New Heart.. 229
Week Thirty-One: Strong Heart.................................. 235
Week Thirty-Two: One Heart 241
Week Thirty-Three: Uncircumcised Heart 247
Week Thirty-Four: Lowly Heart 253
Week Thirty-Five: Good Heart 259
Week Thirty-Six: Overcharged Heart 265
Week Thirty-Seven: Troubled Heart 271
Week Thirty-Eight: Single Heart 277
Week Thirty-Nine: Foolish Heart 283
Week Forty: Impenitent Heart 289
Week Forty-One: Circumcised Heart 295
Week Forty-Two: Evil Heart 301
Week Forty-Three: True Heart 307
Week Forty-Four: Hard Heart..................................... 313
Week Forty-Five: Dark Heart 319
Week Forty-Six: Whorish Heart 325
Week Forty-Seven: Mischievous Heart...................... 331
Week Forty-Eight: Living Heart................................. 337
Week Forty-Nine: Understanding Heart..................... 343
Week Fifty: Covetous Heart 349
Week Fifty-One: Whole Heart.................................... 355
Week Fifty-Two: Whole Heart (II)............................. 361
APPENDIX.. 369
Endnotes.. 393
Other Volumes in the One Heart Series..................... 394

Significance of Day and Time of Devotion

Which Day of the Week to Begin?

Suggestion:

Begin your week on Saturday and follow the Jewish Calendar as oppose to the Gregorian Calendar which we commonly use. Why? There is a blessing in being in step with Gods' timing – it is not about a race of people, but the timing of God. This suggestion is to step into the flow of an anointing that rested on the tribe of Isacchar! It is merely a suggestion, proceed as you desire.

What Time of Day to Begin?

Jesus had a way of saying early in the morning will I seek his face. The day in spiritual terms are divided into 8 watches of 3 hours each. From Sunset to Sunrise, in general 6 p.m. to 6 p.m. the following day.

6 p.m. – 9 p.m.	First Watch
9 p.m. – 12 a.m.	Second Watch
12 a.m. – 3 a.m.	Third Watch
3 a.m. – 6 a.m.	Fourth Watch
6 a.m. – 9 a.m.	Fifth Watch
9 a.m. – 12 p.m.	Sixth Watch
12 p.m. – 3 p.m.	Seventh Watch
3 p.m. – 6 p.m.	Eighth Watch

What Is the Significance of the Time of Day?

Each 3 hour period is called a watch. The First to the Second Watches order your day. The Third to the Fifth Watches REINFORCES the prayer hedges that have been established in the First to Second Watches. The Sixth to the Eighth Watch is being alert and sober awaiting instructions and quenching fiery darts (it is the little foxes that spoil the vine). Get rid of the little foxes that ruin the vineyards as Solomon said in Song of Solomon 2:15

The Danger of Little Things

Excerpt from Bob Gass "On Colorado's long peak, lies the remains of a giant 400-year-old tree. Age, storms, and avalanches, couldn't bring it down. What did? A tiny beetle you could crush under your foot. It ate right through the bark and devoured its heart.

Be careful, it's the little foxes that ruin the vineyards. Little attitudes; but if you practice them often enough, they become fixed attitudes. Little indulgences; but if you give place to them long enough, they desensitize you to sin. Remember when certain things bothered you? Now you don't give them a second thought. You're being desensitized!

Every alcoholic started by telling himself, "I can handle it." Every victim of Internet pornography (and they're getting younger every day), started with a look, got hooked on a fantasy, and ended up uncaging a tiger that:
(a) can devour them; (b) will never willingly go back into its cage.

Before a moral problem got out of hand in the Corinthian church, Paul hit it head on. Listen, "I also received a report...One of your men is sleeping with his step-mother. And you're so above it all that it doesn't even faze you. You pass it off as a small thing, but it's anything but that. Yeast, too, is a 'small thing,' but it works its way through a whole batch...get rid of this 'yeast'" (1Corinthians 5:1-7 TM). Strong language!

Why does God make such a big deal out of this anyway? Because sin hurts us, and anything that hurts one of His children, makes Him angry." You are interacting with others during the Sixth to the Eighth watch that are predominantly outside of your inner circle during the course of a business day. You have prepared yourself to have listening ears, heart and spirit attuned to the voice of God, so when God says move you move, and when God says stop you stop, in other words you are training yourself to walk with God like Enoch and how God intended for us to walk when he created Adam. To meet with him, walk with him in the cool of the day! Walk In the Spirit!

How Do We Walk in the Spirit – Surrendered

Surrender means to yield ownership, to relinquish control over what we consider ours: our property, our time, our "rights."

Stewards over what belongs to someone else – God!

Giving God total control of every jot and tittles of our lives!

It is the Greatest Decision and the Best Decision you will ever make in your life! Your chooser and picker have been broken from birth, and to acknowledge that if we had wanted what he wanted from the beginning our lives would be flawlessly fulfilled! Let Go of Your Way and Take the Assignment of doing it His Way!

Why?

He Loves US and wants what is best for us – our brains weigh science says all of about 3 pounds! How can a finite measurable piece of matter tell the one who measured that matter how their lives should go! How can the clay say to the potter make me this way! Yet He gives us a free will to choose to do it our way, and he will never take that from us! Like the movie star said that he would not let go until they pried it from his cold dead hands, God will let you have it your way like that too!

What are you holding onto like that?

It is your right to do it your way and your freedom of choice? Your right to the pursuit of happiness that the government says you can have? Or some mess you created and called it your world? Are you really happy with the choice you have made so far?

Well if you said no, then let's go about the business of exchanging wills through the way of escape Jesus has made for us as surrendered his right to stay in Heaven and to never die for your sins and mine!

He surrendered more than we will ever surrender! Clearly, he said if we will save our lives we will lose them, but if we will surrender our lives we would gain life! So why not try it this way, His way!

In John 3 Christ choice to surrender His right to be God, again in Matthew 4 and finally He surrendered His right to live for himself! Because he died and rose again and is alive forever more we simply have to give up our way and accept him as our Lord and Savior and believe and have faith in Him and obey the Word of God.

Paul said he died daily to do the will of God and we are no different! To live as He deems for us to live will require a daily decision to wake up and surrender control of your life and choose to walk it out as he has planned!

We are saved, so we have Him as our Savior! Since we have accepted the gift of salvation, have you made him Lord (owner) of your life?

This is where surrender steps in and says I am not my own, but I have been bought with a price and it is my good pleasure to do my masters bidding! Mary Magdalene had the idea when she clinged to Jesus and fell at his feet with gratitude for getting her out of her broken mess she had made from her own decisions!

Jeremiah 29:11 says that God has a plan and a purpose! Don't you want to know what it is?

He will order your steps aright when you determine you want to live your life in his plan and not your own! It will not be comfortable, like breaking in a new pair of shoes it will hurt for a while, but then the shoe surrenders to the shape of your foot or you have to get rid of them or live in pain! Personally, find it difficult to break in new shoes, I look for shoes that are formed the way my foot is formed and spend less time in pain because I am only getting use to the fabric and not the form of the shoe. God has a form for your life and the fabric he wants to adorn you in!

He has the blueprint for your life and the material to build it! His vision sees further down the process than your vision can see "where there is no vision," the people will perish. Where there is limited vision there is obstructions ahead, my paraphrase!

You have one opportunity to get it done! Then after that opportunity comes the judgment! What percentage of Gods plan and purpose for your life will you get accomplished or leave undone and plant in the cemetery! The cemetery is a wealthy place! So many gifted and talented people who died full and not emptied or imparted into the plan of God in the universe!

The calling of God and the gifts are God are without repentance. Let's look at how his word bares out that He is intentional and congruent with his desires for us! His words and his actions line up, that says He wants us to have great success if we would seek him for his way he will not suffer our foot to be moved!

- "Where there is no vision, the people perish." (Proverbs 29:18)

- "For I know the thoughts that I think toward you, says the Lord, thoughts of peace and not of evil, **to give you a future and a hope.**" (Jeremiah 29:11)

- "Your eyes saw my substance, being yet unformed. And in Your book they all were written, the days **fashioned** for me, when as yet there were none of them." (Psalm 139:16)

- "Since his days are **determined**, the number of his months is with You; You have appointed his limits, so that he cannot pass." (Job 14:5)

- "And we know that all things work together for good to those who love God, to those who are called **according to His purpose.**" (Romans 8:28)

- "For many are called, but few are chosen." (Matthew 22:14)

Determined and fashioned" plans for as long as the earth remaineth, and seedtime and harvest! Heaven and Earth will pass away, but his Word will be forever! You and I will pass away, but His Word, His Will for his creation will never change! What a plan!

Do you still want to sing "I Did It My Way"?

The blind leading the blind - when He promises to give us sight that exceeds natural abilities by being a lamp unto our feet and a light unto our pathway! He will order your steps on every hand; from marriage, careers and ministry! We have compassed this same mountain long enough don't you think? It is time to go up and possess the land!

Caleb and Joshua said they were well able to go up when God first told them that the land was theirs, but because they were surrounded by wavering and self-willed people they had to wait for them to vanquish in the way they chose over the way God had chosen for them!

When they did go up to possess the land they got the directions right and got there and discovered that the people the others had thought would see them as grasshoppers, had been living in fear of them all of those years because they had heard how God had brought them out of the land of Egypt!

They had expected them 40 years sooner to come in and depose them from the land! How long will we stand halted between two opinions? If God is God then serve Him!

The Bible says that unless God builds the "house" we will labor in vain trying to do it all on our own. Foundations are laid by God that we see in Isaiah where he made highways in the wilderness so that the animals would not devour them! How does this happen? When our wills are surrendered to the point where God can create and birth in us his divine plan!

- "For as many are led by the Spirit of God, these are the sons of God." (Romans 8:14)

- "The steps of a good man are ordered by the Lord ..." (Psalm 37:23)

- "O Lord, I know the way of a man is not in himself; it is not in man who walks to direct his own steps." (Jeremiah 10:23)

- "There is a way which seems right to a man, but its end is the way of death." (Proverbs 14:12)

- "A man's steps are of the Lord. How then can a man understand his own way?" (Proverbs 20:24)

- "A man's heart plans his way, but the Lord directs his steps." (Proverbs 16:9)

- "Direct my steps by Your word, and let no iniquity have dominion over me." (Psalm 119:133)

- "Therefore be followers of God as dear children." (Ephesians 5:1)

- "My sheep hear My voice, and I know them, and they follow Me." (John 10:27)

- "Trust in the Lord with all your heart, and lean not on your own understanding; in all your ways acknowledge Him, and He shall direct your paths." (Proverbs 3:5)

- "The Lord is my Shepherd; I shall not want. He makes me to lie down in green pastures; He leads me beside the still waters. He restores my soul; He leads me in the paths of righteousness for His name's sake." (Psalm 23:1)

- Thus says the Lord, your Redeemer, the Holy One of Israel: "I am the Lord your God, who teaches you to profit, who leads you by the way you should go." (Isaiah 48:17)

- "Show me Your ways, O Lord; teach me Your paths. Lead me in Your truth and teach me, for You are the God of my salvation ..." (Psalm 25:4)

- "I will instruct you and teach you in the way you should go; I will guide you with My eye." (Psalm 32:8)

- "Teach me Your way, O Lord, and lead me in a smooth path, because of my enemies." (Psalm 27:11)

- "The Lord will guide you continually ..." (Isaiah 58:11)

- "For this is God, our God forever and ever; He will be our guide even to death." (Psalm 48:14)

- "Moreover You led them by day with a cloudy pillar, and by night with a pillar of fire, to give them light on the road which they should travel." (Nehemiah 9:12)

- "All we like sheep have gone astray; we have turned, every one, to his own way ..." (Isaiah 53:6)

- "Therefore you shall be careful to do as the Lord Your God has commanded you; You shall not turn aside to the right hand or to the left." (Deuteronomy 5:32)

We become Sons of God when we are:

- Led by the Spirit of God

- The steps of a good man are ordered by the Lord

- It is not in man who walks to direct his own steps

- A way which seems right to a man ... its end is the way of death

- A man's steps are of the Lord

- The Lord directs his steps

- Direct my steps by Your Word

- Be followers of God as dear children

- My sheep hear My voice ... and they follow Me
- He shall direct your paths
- He leads me by still waters
- He leads me in the paths of righteousness
- Leads you by the way you should go
- Lead me in your truth
- I will guide you with My eye
- Lead me in a smooth path
- The Lord will guide you continually
- He will be our guide even to death
- Led them by day ... to give them light on the road which they should travel

"Neither Wast Thou Washed...[Nor] Salted...Nor Swaddled." Ezekiel 16:4

(1) You must be washed by "the washing of water by the Word" (Eph 5:26)

(2) You must be salted as a newborn baby was in Jewish tradition rubbed with salt to toughen their skins and to prevent bruising – reducing the need for "special handling."

(3) You must be swaddled - covered and protected through fellowship that holds you accountable to remain committed to God.

A few names of some who suffered dire consequences for not surrendering totally to follow God:

Adam, Eve, Cain, Moses, Jacob and David

Why have we as Christians not entered into our Promised Land on Earth! I find no fault in God, but in us as Christians! It is a place to be entered into by following the directions completely!

1. "Surely none of the men who came up from Egypt, from twenty years old and above, shall see the land of which I swore to Abraham, Isaac, and Jacob, because they have not wholly followed Me, 'except Caleb ... and Joshua ... for they have wholly followed the Lord.' " "So the Lord's anger was aroused against Israel, and He made them wander in the wilderness forty years, until all the generation that had done evil in the sight of the Lord was gone." (Numbers 32:11)

2. Then the Lord said: "I have pardoned, according to your word ... because all these men who have seen My glory and the signs which I did in Egypt and in the wilderness, and have put Me to the test now these ten times, and have not heeded My voice, they certainly shall not see the land of which I swore to their fathers, nor shall any of those who rejected Me see it. But My servant Caleb, because he has a different spirit in him and has followed Me fully, I will bring into the land where he went, and his descendants shall inherit it." (Numbers 14:20)

Those who follow their way are disobedient and eat the fruit of their desires:

1. "Woe to the rebellious children," says the Lord, "Who take counsel, but not of Me, and who devise plans, but not of My Spirit, that they may add sin to sin; who walk to go down to Egypt, and have not asked My advice, to strengthen themselves in the strength of Pharaoh, and to trust in the shadow of Egypt! Therefore the strength of Pharaoh shall be your shame, and trust in the shadow of Egypt shall be your humiliation." (Isaiah 30:1)

2. "If you are willing and obedient, you shall eat the good of the land; but if you refuse and rebel, you shall be devoured by the sword;" for the mouth of the Lord has spoken. (Isaiah 1:19)

Be not deceived God is not mocked, what we sow we shall reap! When we do it our way we live generationally under the consequences. Choices made in our teens become a foundation that we have our house – built on, and if it was shaky then we tend to have unstable houses!

God is a rewarder of those who diligently seek Him and intend to be led by Him!

- "For what is a man profited if he gains the whole world, and loses his own soul? For the Son of Man ... will reward each according to his works." (Matthew 16:26)

- "... and each one will receive his own reward according to his own labor." (1 Corinthians 3:8)

- "And behold, I am coming quickly, and My reward is with Me, to give to every one according to his work." (Revelation 22:12)

- "... I am He who searches the minds and hearts. And I will give to each one according to your works." (Revelation 2:23)

- "For the Son of Man will come in the glory of His Father with His angels, and then He will reward each according to his works." (Matthew 16:27)

- "And everyone who has left houses or brothers or sisters or father or mother or wife or children or lands, for My name's sake, shall receive a hundredfold, and inherit everlasting life." (Matthew 19:29)

The Word of God says that it is appointed unto man, once to die and then the judgment! When you die how will you be judged?

1. "Let us hear the conclusion of the whole matter: Fear God and keep His commandments, for this is the whole duty of man. For God will bring every work into judgment, including every secret thing, whether it is good or whether it is evil." (Ecclesiastes 12:13)

2. "And there is no creature hidden from His sight, but all things are naked and open to the eyes of Him to whom we must give account." (Hebrews 4:13)

3. "For we must all appear before the judgment seat of Christ, that each one may receive the things done in the body, according to what he has done, whether good or bad." (2 Corinthians 5:10)

Are you ready to surrender?

Circle Your Answer:

YES   NO

And then be prepared to live with the consequences!

If you answered YES, let's go further! If you answered NO - come on and go along anyway – what do you have to lose?

What man builds a house without first counting up the cost?

Well it will cost you something either way!

Surrender is the Way to GO!

NO turning back – no matter what comes or goes – don't look back and become like Lots' wife!

For full surrender and commitment to God you must make a quality decision to face life and its circumstances, and test head on without crumbling in the face of adversity. Your face must be like flint unmoved by the changes around you, draw a line in the sand and declare and decree that you are marching forward and not move backwards. Your determination will be tested, your loyalty will be mocked and your faith tested in the furnace of affliction.

Count it all as dung for the prize that is set before you, no matter how hard pressed you are on every side the race will not be given to the swift but to the one who endures to the end!

This fight is a fight where there will be only one winner and you must determine that will be you!

Total surrender requires totally relying on God to lead, guide and order your life according to his good pleasure!

Whatever "measure" you use – is measured back to you. Give him 1/3 of your life and that is what you will have in return! He will give you back what you give Him!

Surrender and sanctification is required on the following levels by Jehovah M'Kaddesh which encompasses your whole self from beginning to end!

Your Physical, Spiritual and Emotional being will be sanctified thoroughly!

Paul explains Jehovah M'Kaddesh in I Thessalonians 5:23 "Now may the God of peace Himself sanctify you completely; and may your whole spirit, soul, and body be preserved blameless at the coming of our Lord Jesus Christ." (1 Thessalonians 5:23)

First –

We must Pray!

Father,

In the name of Jesus, I fully surrender physically, spiritually and emotionally to your will for my life! Give me directions for your divine will for my life and order my steps in Your Word! Sanctify me from the roots of my tree and lead me beside still waters and restore my soul, and lead me in a plain path! I thank you and praise you for all that you have done, are doing and going to do in my life in Jesus Name, Amen!

Next,

Secondly –

We must Pray that we will remain!

Father,

In the name of Jesus, I have surrendered my whole self to you from now until eternity and I believe that you will not allow me to go astray, but lead me in the plain path of righteousness that you have designed and fashioned for me from the time you had me on your mind! I thank you and praise you for keeping me, because I desire to be kept! In Jesus Name, Amen!

What does God think about your choice?

"Unless the Lord builds the house, they labor in vain who build it." (Psalm 127:1)

What does God say about being Lord of your life?

"Therefore whoever hears these sayings of Mine, and does them, I will liken him to a wise man who built his house on the rock; and the rain descended, the floods came, and the winds blew and beat on that house; and it did not fall, for it was founded on the rock. Now everyone who hears these sayings of Mine, and does not do them, will be like a foolish man who built his house on the sand: and the rain descended, the floods came, and the winds blew and beat on that house, and it fell. And great was its fall." (Matthew 7:24)

How Does God Reward Your Choice?

"... I have set before you life and death, blessing and cursing; therefore choose life, that both you and your descendants may live, that you may love the Lord your God, that you may obey His voice, and that you may cling to Him, for He is your life and the length of your days ..." (Deuteronomy 30:19)

Naturally you will try to get back on the throne of your life, and perhaps you will! But you now know the way down off the throne! I Beseech YOU by the Mercies of God through Christ Jesus that you run the race that is before you and not turn around and lose ground – in the name of Jesus! AMEN!

Why? Paul is about to tell you – "For though I am free from all men, I have made myself a servant to all, that I might win the more." (1 Corinthians 9:19) You were bought at a price; do not become slaves of men. Brethren, let each one remain with God in that calling in which he was called." (1 Corinthians 7:23)

How will you know you are progressing?

- You shall know a tree by the fruit it bears!

There are 9 Parts to the Fruit of the Spirit:

Galatians 5:22 "But the fruit of the Spirit, is love, joy, peace, longsuffering, gentleness, goodness, faith, meekness, temperance, against such there is no law."

There Are 17 Works Of The Flesh:

So Galatians 5:1 says, "Stand fast therefore in the liberty, wherewith Christ hath made us free, and be not entangled again with the yoke of bondage. In this case unforgiveness!

Galatians 5:16, says "Walk (follow) in the spirit, and ye shall not fulfill the lust of the flesh.

How do you walk in the spirit? Someone asked how do you eat an elephant, and the response was "One bite at a time." So take a bite of the fruit of the spirit one bite at a time until you have eaten the whole fruit!

If not, you will work harder in Satan's camp than you ever will in God's! Now let's follow Christ day-by-day!

Repentance

1 Come, and let us return unto the LORD: for he hath torn, and he will heal us; he hath smitten, and he will bind us up. 2 After two days will he revive us: in the third day he will raise us up, and we shall live in his sight. 3 Then shall we know, if we follow on to know the LORD: his going forth is prepared as the morning; and he shall come unto us as the rain, as the latter and former rain unto the earth. HOSEA Chapter 6:1-3 (KJV)

Love

This word seems to require explanation only in the case of its use by our Lord in his interview with "Simon, the son of Jonas," after his resurrection (John 21:16, 17). When our Lord says, "Lovest thou me?" he uses the Greek word _agapas_; and when Simon answers, he uses the Greek word _philo_, i.e., "I love." This is the usage in the first and second questions put by our Lord; but in the third our Lord uses Simon's word. The distinction between these two Greek words is thus fitly described by Trench:, "_Agapan_ has more of judgment and deliberate choice; _philein_ has more of attachment and peculiar personal affection. Thus the 'Lovest thou' (Gr. agapas) on the lips of the Lord seems to Peter at this moment too cold a word, as though his Lord were keeping him at a distance, or at least not inviting him to draw near, as in the passionate yearning of his heart he desired now to do. Therefore he puts by the word and substitutes his own stronger 'I love' (Gr. philo) in its room. A second time he does the same. And now he has conquered; for when the Lord demands a third time whether he loves him, he does it in the word which alone will satisfy Peter ('Lovest thou,' Gr. phileis), which alone claims from him that personal attachment and affection with which indeed he knows that his heart is full."

In 1Corinthians 13 the apostle sets forth the excellency of love, as the word "charity" there is rendered in the Revised Version.

—Easton's Illustrated Dictionary

Weekly Plan Outline: Day 1

Saturday Remember Put on Your Armour!

Begin the Week by telling yourself and God the truth about where you are in your heart today! Then face that truth no matter how ugly it is. Repent and commit it to God. Why tell God the truth – doesn't he already know – you are wondering? Yes he does know, but this is about you and with the mouth confession is made unto salvation! Confession is with the intent to become transparent and removing the cloak of shame from your heart!

DAILY
Put on the Whole Armour as a Lifestyle!

Helmet of Salvation
to keep my thoughts aligned with your will

Loins Girt with Truth
to keep me in integrity

Breastplate of Righteousness protect my standing in the community

Gospel of Peace
to order my steps correctly

Shield of Faith
to secure my purpose and destiny

Sword of the Spirit
to reign, rule and have dominion

Weekly Plan Outline: Day 2

Sunday Remember Put on Your Armour!

Pray Psalms 51 in the first person tense for yourself, no matter who has hurt or betrayed you. What role did you play in what happened to you, perhaps you were an innocent child, or a willing participant until things went sour -- what happened to cause your heart to be broken. Admit blame if there is any, because if you had a choice to stay in a bad relationship or go, and you chose to stay -- take responsibility for that part. If you were an innocent child or youth, how has what happened to you affected your today -- are you still a victim of the predator. Today you can choose by faith to no longer be the victim -- one day, one minute, one second at a time until you are completely free in Jesus Name! This is a universal truth, 'For every cause there is a reaction.' We are responsible for the decisions we make and the relationships we entertain. Perhaps you were violated physically, emotionally, sexually and socially -- all without cause, but God has made a way of escape for you from all of these violations! Forgive! He doesn't want you walking around with the aftermath of the wars that have been waged against you as a badge of honor. Whatever it was -- you are still here, and God is still able!

Psalms 119:165 says we are to take no offense. When we take offense we take that person who offended us and tie them to our bodies and carry them around as weights. Weights that prevent us from entering into the doors of blessings God has prepared for us. Unlatch the bodies so you can enter into the rest of God for your soul, and be healed in the name of the Lord!

Weekly Plan Outline: Day 3
Monday Remember Put on Your Armour!

Continue as an action of intent to forgive. Forgiveness is not a feeling -- but a commandment (to do). Release yourself from the torment, you deserve it. Pray "By faith (trust in God's ability) I choose to forgive those who have caused me pain in Jesus Name. I forgive name them as an act of faith. You may be feeling anger, rage, teeth grinding and fist clenching emotions rise up inside. So, in the name of Jesus I speak peace to your spirit, soul, mind and body. I bind you Satan from the heart of this one. I command you to release this one now in the name of Jesus! Amen! Father give your angels charge over them to preserve them during this time of pain! Now! Thank God for peace, joy, grace, and forgiveness. Ask him to wash you and purge you with hyssop. Confess this scripture. "Behold, thou desirest truth in the inward parts: and in the hidden part thou shalt make me to know wisdom. Make me to hear joy and gladness: that the bones which thou has broken may rejoice. Hide thy face from my sins, and blot out all mine iniquities, Create in a me a clean heart, O God, and renew a right spirit within me. Cast me not away from thy presence; and take not thy holy spirit from me. Restore unto me the joy of thy salvation; and uphold me with thy free spirit." (Psalms 51:6-12)

Weekly Plan Outline: Day 4
Tuesday Remember Put on Your Armour!

Begin thanking God for restoring your peace and his forgiveness because you held onto unforgiveness in your heart. Satan knows we must forgive so he impedes us with a belief we have a right to unforgiveness! To obtain the blessings He desires to bestow on us we must be broken. Brokenness in its' purest form is to desire to walk in God's perfect will for your life. The safest place in the world is in the arms of Jesus, a songwriter penned! How we handle what has happened to us and who did things to us will determine how the anointing will be able to flow through us! Unforgiveness causes spiritual blockage! God's grace is sufficient in all times, all seasons of your life as a vessel that has been damaged by the warfare of life waged against, comes traumas aftermath; shame, humiliation and other collateral damages. Despair not! Remember "What shall we say to these things? (rape, murder, persecution, rejections on every hand, etc.) If God be for us.... Then what shall separate us from the love of Christ? ...tribulation, distress, persecution, famine, nakedness, peril, nor sword?...I am persuaded, that neither death, life, angels, principalities, powers, things present, things to come, height, depth, nor creature, shall separate us from the love of God, which is in Christ Jesus our Lord. (Romans 8:31-39)

Weekly Plan Outline: Day 5
Wednesday Remember Put on Your Armour!

But God has made a way of escape through his son Jesus Christ! "There hath no temptation taken you but such as is common to man; but God is faithful, who will not suffer you to be tempted above that ye are able, but with the temptation also make a way of escape, that ye may be able to bear it. Wherefore my dearly beloved, flee from idolatry. (I Corinthians 10:13-14) Anything that occupies the space in our heart the belongs to God is idolatry. The issues of the past that we nurse, are a form of idolatry -- and the pain has become our God. We feed the pain medications, alcohol and illicit relationships in an effort to appease the beast! But remember not to be entangled again with the yoke of bondage. Every time you feel that pain returning, or resurfacing as you see the person or persons who caused you pain -- remember to forgive by faith until it becomes manifested. That is faith, it is the evidence of things hoped for and the evidence of things not seen. You reach for it, grab hold of it and hold onto it until it manifest itself as yours. At this point I want you to see that the person and the spirit behind the person who hurt you are two separate issues. Under the control of Satan the person(s) or persons did to you what they would not have done to themselves. Can't you see how Satan is the originator of abuse. He promises people fame and fortune, uses them and discards them when he is finished destroying them. He is a father who abuses his own children. Allow God to pour out your heart in mercy to the one who mistreated you, and pray for God to send laborers in their path to release them from the snare of Satan. God does not expect you to embrace your perpetrator in any form. What he does require is obedience to His will! I say this because there are those who have harmed me that God asked me if I would write a letter to them expressing what affect their crime had on my life, and then to go so far as to personally stand before them and confront them with the crime! God deals with us individually as he knows us better than we know ourselves! I am not recommending you do the same, because without God's leading you may find yourself in harms way! If there is no peace in the instructions you are about to embark on – then do not pursue! David inquired of God "shall I pursue" and God said "Yes" in addition to Yes he said he would give them into his hands to overtake! When God says pursue that is when you pursue! OTHERWISE STAND DOWN! Because God will right every wrong! It is yours to forgive and Gods' to revenge!

When Jesus died on the Cross of Calvary and uttered with his lips to His Father to forgive his perpetrators – he made provision for an anointing if you would a gift of forgiveness to be accessible to every believer when faced with such crisis. It is up to us to access that anointing, because he will not force it on you! God gives us the grace to forgive through the final breath that was on Jesus' lips while on the cross. "Father forgive, them for they know not what they do." Through all the things that Satan meant for evil to destroy you, God has turned and is turning them around for your good. Since, you are reading this book it is evident that the hardship did not destroy you! Maybe it did someone else you know, but GODhas a plan! In Jeremiah 29:11 He says "For I know the thoughts that I think towards you, saith the Lord, thoughts of peace, and not of evil, to give you an expected end." Evil lies in the heart of men and they choose to hurt by free will, yielding their members as instruments of evil. But because God who at all times kept you on every hand from losing your mind. You are still here to turn around and bruise the head of Satan for what he has done to you and your family. I am still here to tell you that God is a restoring God and that He will repay the evil that has been done to you. The people who allowed Satan to use them, are of all people most miserable. May not look like it on the outside, but on the inside it is an ugly state of being. They have to not only bear the mark of what they did, but they have to face God's judgment! Pray to the Lord of the Harvest to send someone to lead them home! Because we are to pray for our enemies! Not because we want to see them go free of any penalties, that is not your place! God said the wages of sin are death, there is spiritual death that exist among the living! Some of your perpertrators called themselves Christians, and I say called themselves! Gods' Word clearly tells us that many call on his name but their hearts are far from him! Being the Judge and Jury sentences you to a state of deadness! It is difficult for you to get the full measure of living out of your life, because death is laying in the midst of your heart!

Weekly Plan Outline: Day 6
Thursday Remember Put on Your Armour!

Could you be the one to share the gospel with them and save them from a burning hell. If that seems farfetched to you, I understand, but I promise you it can happen, and has happened! Remember one plants, another waters, and God gives the increase! Again this is not an expectation from God in the natural! To accomplish this God would have to place an anointing on you that would empower you to witness to someone who has injured you without malice in your heart! Only Pursue When GOD says Pursue!

You don't have to get up close and personal. God knows the wound is fresh. You could opt to send what I will call a 'Salvation Letter' and tell the individual(s) how you feel and let them know that God has been faithful to relieve you of the weight of what was done to you by them without a return address. And that you would like to extend that same offer to them. Tell them you forgave them by faith, and that God will forgiven them, and help them to forgive themselves too. Tell them you love them through Christ Jesus. God teaches us how to love the unlovely, because we too were once unlovely and guilty of death.

Weekly Plan Outline: Day 7
Friday Remember Put on Your Armour!

The number of Perfection. " Being confident of this very thing that, He who hath begun a good work in you (is able to) will perform it until the day of Jesus Christ." (Philippians 1:6) Today is fruit picking day. What fruit can you pick from the Tree of Life to feed your heart today. Choose one or two and get started eating the scriptures that apply to that particular fruit. You have emptied out the works of the flesh from your heart, and that requires that you put something in its place to prevent the crop from returning 7 fold. This number we call perfection comes forth as we are shaken to the very core of our being! During years with the number 7 on them I have found myself personally in a season of conflicting moments! It is like a Charles Dickens – Tale of Two Cities (It was the best of times and the worst of times) all at the same time! How could you be in such crisis on one hand, have a thunderstorm on one side of your life and the Sun shining on the other side! Well it is called life, but it is also a time that comes when God needs to see if He can trust you with His Blessings! Will you turn back at the least bit of distressing moments, or will you set your face like flint and declare that as for me and my house we will serve the Lord! I will not look back like Lots wife, and I will not be denied like Moses' at the mouth of the manifestation of the promises of God in my life! Whatever has happened to you up to now – God says is no comparison to what he has in store for those who love him and are called according to his purpose! It is his desire that you be in health, and prosper even as your soul prospers.

What is the Heart: Holman

The center of the physical, mental, and spiritual life of humans. This contrasts to the normal use of kardia ("heart") in Greek literature outside the Scriptures. The New Testament follows the Old Testament usage when referring to the human heart in that it gives kardia a wider range of meaning than it was generally accustomed to have.

First, the word heart refers to the physical organ and is considered to be the center of the physical life. Eating and drinking are spoken of as strengthening the heart (Genesis 18:5; Judges 19:5; Acts 14:17). As the center of physical life, the heart came to stand for the person as a whole. The heart became the focus for all the vital functions of the body; including both intellectual and spiritual life. The heart and the intellect are closely connected, the heart being the seat of intelligence: "For this people's heart is waxed gross... lest at any time they should... understand with their heart, and should be converted" (Matthew 13:15). The heart is connected with thinking: As a person "thinketh in his heart, so is he" (Proverbs 23:7). To ponder something in one's heart means to consider it carefully (Luke 1:66; Luke 2:19). "To set one's heart on" is the literal Hebrew that means to give attention to something, to worry about it (1 Samuel 9:20). To call to heart (mind) something means to remember something (Isaiah 46:8). All of these are functions of the mind, but are connected with the heart in biblical language. Closely related to the mind are acts of the will, acts resulting from a conscious or even a deliberate decision. Thus, 2 Corinthians 9:7: "Every man according as he purposeth in his heart, so let him give." Ananias contrived his deed of lying to the Holy Spirit in his heart (Acts 5:4). The conscious decision is made in the heart (Romans 6:17). Connected to the will are human wishes and desires. Romans 1:24 describes how God gave them up "through the lusts of their own hearts, to dishonor their own bodies." David was a man after God's "own heart" because he would "fulfill all" of God's will (Acts 13:22). Not only is the heart associated with the activities of the mind and the will, but it is also closely connected to the feelings and affections of a person. Emotions such as joy originate in the heart (Psalms 4:7; Isaiah 65:14). Other emotions are ascribed to the heart, especially in the Old Testament. Nabal's fear is described by the phrase: "his heart died within him" (1 Samuel 25:37; compare Psalms 143:4). Discouragement or despair is described by the phrase "heaviness in the heart" which makes it stoop (Proverbs 12:25). Again, Ecclesiastes 2:20 says, "Therefore I went about to cause my heart to despair of all the labor which I took under the sun." Another emotion connected with the heart is sorrow. John 16:6 says, "because I have said these things unto you, sorrow hath filled your heart." Proverbs 25:20, describes sorrow as having "an heavy heart." The heart is also the seat of the affection of love and its opposite, hate. In the Old Testament, for example, Israel is commanded: "You shall not hate your brother in your heart, but you shall reason with your neighbor, lest you bear sin because of him" (Leviticus 19:17 RSV). A similar attitude, bitter jealousy, is described in James 3:14 as coming from the heart. On the other hand, love is based in the heart. The believer is commanded to love God "with all your heart" (Mark 12:30; compare Deuteronomy 6:5). Paul taught that the purpose of God's command is love which comes from a "pure heart" (1 Timothy 1:5). Finally, the heart is spoken of in Scripture as the center of the moral and spiritual life. The conscience, for instance, is associated with the heart. In fact, the Hebrew language had no word for conscience, so the word heart was often used to express this concept: "my heart shall not reproach me so long as I live" (Job 27:6). The Revised Standard Version translates the word for "heart" as "conscience" in 1 Samuel 25:31 (RSV). In the New Testament the heart is spoken of also as that which condemns us (1 John 3:19-21). All moral conditions from the highest to the lowest are said to center in the heart. Sometimes the heart is used to represent a person's true nature or character. Samson told Delilah "all his heart" (Judges 16:17). This true nature is contrasted with the outward appearance: "man looks on the outward appearance, but the Lord looks on the heart" (1 Samuel 16:7 RSV). On the negative side, depravity is said to issue from the heart: "The heart is deceitful above all things, and desperately wicked: who can know it?" (Jeremiah 17:9). Jesus said that out of the heart comes evil thoughts, murder, adultery, fornication, theft, false witness, slander (Matthew 15:19). In other words, defilement comes from within rather than from without. Because the heart is at the root of the problem, this is the place where God does His work in the individual. For instance, the work of the law is "written in their hearts," and conscience is the proof of this (Romans 2:15). The heart is the field where seed (the Word of God) is sown (Matthew 13:19; Luke 8:15). In addition to being the place where the natural laws of God are written, the heart is the place of renewal. Before Saul became king, God gave him a new heart (1 Samuel 10:9). God promised Israel that He would give them a new spirit within, take away their "stony heart" and give them a "heart of flesh" (Ezekiel 11:19). Paul said that a person must believe in the heart to be saved, "for with the heart man believeth unto righteousness" (Romans 10:10). (See also Mark 11:23; Hebrews 3:12.) Finally, the heart is the dwelling place of God. Two persons of the

Trinity are said to reside in the heart of the believer. God has given us the "earnest of the Spirit in our hearts" (2 Corinthians 1:22). Ephesians 3:17 expresses the desire that "Christ may dwell in your hearts by faith." The love of God "is shed abroad in our hearts by the Holy Ghost which is given unto us" (Romans 5:5).

Holman Bible Dictionary, published by Broadman & Holman, 1991. All rights reserved. Used by permission of Broadman & Holman. By Gerald Cowen

What is The Heart: Faussets

Often including the intellect as well as the affections and will; as conversely the "mind" often includes the feeling and will as well as the intellect. Romans 1:21, "their foolish heart was darkened." Ephesians 1:18, "the eyes of your understanding (the Vaticanus manuscript; but the Sinaiticus and Alexandrinus manuscripts 'heart') being enlightened." Thus, the Scripture implies that the heart and the head act and react on one another; and in men's unbelief it is the will that perverts the intellectual perceptions. John 7:17, "if any man be willing to (Greek) do, he shall know." "Willingness to obey" is the key to spiritual knowledge. See Jeremiah 17:9; Hosea 7:11, "Ephraim is like a silly dove without heart," i.e. "moral understanding".

The Heart: Old Testament Hebrew Lexicon

1. inner man, mind, will, heart, understanding
    a. inner part, midst
        1. midst (of things)
        2. heart (of man)
        3. soul, heart (of man)
        4. mind, knowledge, thinking, reflection, memory
        5. inclination, resolution, determination (of will)
        6. conscience
        7. heart (of moral character)
        8. as seat of appetites
        9. as seat of emotions and passions, as the seat of courage

Heart, appears in the Old Testament throughout the books, but the most recorded of 99 times in the Psalms!

The Renewed Heart: Torrey's Topical Textbook
It is a place when renewed will do the following:

- Prepared to seek God 2 Chronicles 19:3; Ezra 7:10; Psalms 10:17
- Fixed on God Psalms 57:7; 112:7
- Joyful in God 1 Samuel 2:1; Zechariah 10:7
- Perfect with God 1 Kings 8:61; Psalms 101:2
- Upright Psalms 97:11; 125:4
- Clean Psalms 73:1
- Pure Psalms 24:4; Matthew 5:8
- Tender 1 Samuel 24:5; 2 Kings 22:19
- Single and sincere Acts 2:46; Hebrews 10:22
- Honest and good Luke 8:15
- Broken, contrite Psalms 34:18; 51:17
- Obedient Psalms 119:112; Romans 6:17
- Filled with the law of God Psalms 40:8; 119:11
- Awed by the word of God Psalms 119:161
- Filled with the fear of God Jeremiah 32:40
- Meditative Psalms 4:4; 77:6
- Circumcised Deuteronomy 30:6; Romans 2:29
- Void of fear Psalms 27:3
- Desirous of God Psalms 84:2
- Enlarged Psalms 119:32; 2 Corinthians 6:11
- Faithful to God Nehemiah 9:8
- Confident in God Psalms 112:7
- Sympathizing Jeremiah 4:19; Lamentations 3:51
- Prayerful 1 Samuel 1:13; Psalms 27:8
- Inclined to Obedience Psalms 119:112
- Wholly devoted to God Psalms 9:1; 119:10,69,145
- Zealous 2 Chronicles 17:6; Jeremiah 20:9
- Wise Proverbs 10:8; 14:33; 23:15
- A treasury of good Matthew 12:35

The Unrenewed Heart: Torrey's Topical Textbook
It is a place when unrenewed will do the following:
- Hateful to God Proverbs 6:16,18; 11:20
- Full of evil Ecclesiastes 9:3
- Full of evil imaginations Genesis 6:5; 8:21; Proverbs 6:18
- Full of vain thoughts Jeremiah 4:14
- Fully set to do evil Ecclesiastes 8:11
- Desperately wicked Jeremiah 17:9
- Far from God Isaiah 29:13; Matthew 15:8
- Not perfect with God 1 Kings 15:3; Acts 8:21; Proverbs 6:18
- Not prepared to seek God 2 Chronicles 12:14
- A treasury of evil Matthew 12:35; Mark 7:21
- Darkened Romans 1:21
- Prone to error Psalms 95:10
- Prone to depart from God Deuteronomy 29:18; Jeremiah 17:5
- Impenitent Romans 2:5
- Unbelieving Hebrews 3:12
- Blind Ephesians 4:18
- Uncircumcised Leviticus 26:41; Acts 7:51
- Of little worth Proverbs 10:20
- Deceitful Jeremiah 17:9
- Deceived Isaiah 44:20; James 1:26
- Divided Hosea 10:2
- Double 1 Chronicles 12:33; Psalms 12:2
- Hard Ezekiel 3:7; Mark 10:5; Romans 2:5
- Haughty Proverbs 18:12; Jeremiah 48:29
- Influenced by the devil John 13:2
- Carnal Romans 8:7
- Covetous Jeremiah 22:17; 2 Peter 2:14
- Despiteful Ezekiel 25:15
- Ensnaring Ecclesiastes 7:26

- Foolish Proverbs 12:23; 22:15
- Froward Psalms 101:4; Proverbs 6:14; 17:20
- Fretful against the Lord Proverbs 19:3
- Idolatrous Ezekiel 14:3,4
- Mad Ecclesiastes 9:3
- Mischievous Psalms 28:3; 140:2
- Proud Psalms 101:5; Jeremiah 49:16
- Rebellious Jeremiah 5:23
- Perverse Proverbs 12:8
- Stiff Ezekiel 2:4
- Stony Ezekiel 11:19; 36:26
- Stout Isaiah 10:12; 46:12
- Elated by sensual indulgence Hosea 13:3
- Elated by prosperity 2 Chronicles 26:16; Daniel 5:20
- Studies destruction Proverbs 24:2
- Often judicially stupefied Isaiah 6:10; Acts 28:26,27
- Often judicially hardened Exodus 4:21; Joshua 11:20

Some Heart Types in the Bible
God Prefers: Spirit-Led (Positive) 26

Grieved Heart	Genesis 6:6	Pure Heart	Psalm 24:4
Willing Heart	Exodus 25:2	Broken Heart	Psalm 34:18
Stirred Heart	Exodus 35:35	Panting Heart	Psalm 38:10
Another Heart	I Samuel 10:9	Failing Heart	Psalm 40:12
Perfect Heart	I Chronicles 12:38	Proclaiming Heart	Psalm 45:1
Tender Heart	II Chronicles 34:27	Established Fixed Heart	Psalm 57:7
Sorrowful Heart	Nehemiah 2:2-12	Living Heart	Psalm 69:32
Faithful Heart	Nehemiah 9:8	Established Heart	Psalm 112:8
Soft Heart	Job 23:16	Understanding Heart	Proverbs 2:2
Upright Heart	Job 33:3	Retaining Heart	Proverbs 4:4,21
Communing Heart	Psalm 4:4	Sound Heart	Proverbs 14:30
Heart of Wax	Psalm 22:14	Merry Heart	Proverbs 17:22
Wise Heart	Exodus 35:35	New Heart	Ezekiel 18:31 36:26

Some Heart Types in the Bible cont'd
God Despises: Flesh-Led (Negative) 25

Evil Heart	Genesis 6:5	Fat Greasy Heart	Psalm 119:70
Hardened Heart	Exodus 4:21	Desolate Heart	Psalm 143:4
Deceived Heart	Deuteronomy 11:16	Despising Heart	Proverbs 5:12
Non-Perceiving Heart	Deuteronomy 29:4	Deceitful Heart	Proverbs 12:20
Proud Heart	Psalm 101:5	Bitter Heart	Proverbs 14:10
Presumptuous Heart	Esther 7:5	Backslidden Heart	Proverbs 14:14
Hypocritical Heart	Job 36:13	Foolish Heart	Proverbs 15:7
Lifted-up Heart	Deuteronomy 8:14	Human Heart	Proverbs 15:11
Firm, Hard Heart	Job 41:24	Abominable Heart	Proverbs 26:25
Iniquitous Heart	Psalm 41:6	Double Heart	James 1:8
Wicked Heart	Psalm 58:2	Wounded Heart	Psalm 109:22
Erring Heart	Psalm 95:10	Evil Heart	Matthew 15:19
		Rebellious Heart	Jeremiah 5:23

Buried Alive

A voice of a young man called out to me in the distance as I was walking in the botanical gardens. I love walking in the gardens because of the smell and the sights. The garden was full of freshly cut green grass and the sight of new life blossoming on stately stems of green; painted against the baby blue horizon of a midday spring sky. How fresh it all makes me feel, but this voice kept calling out to me from the distance; breaking into the serenity that I had found. Turning in the direction of the voice the words were faint but the closer I came to the voice it became clearer. So clear that the words begin to manifest and the words was "Help Me"! It was as if he knew I was passing by or maybe not. As I looked for the body to go with the voice and the cry for help frantically now, because the sounds of "Help Me" were getting louder! I felt compelled not to say a word to keep from drowning out his cries. Just as I came to where it seemed the voice was coming from, it stopped suddenly! Oh no I said inside of myself, do not stop now I am here; softly I asked him where he was! He said down here, and my eyes turned downward and yet saw nothing but the plush grass beneath my feet!

Quickly, where are you I asked? He responded - down here! By this time, my patience was on the brink of collapse as I still saw no visible sign of anyone being beneath my feet. The ground I stood on was smooth, clean, and undisturbed from all appearances. Again, he began to say those words frantically "Help Me"!

I dropped to my knees, placed my ear against the ground, called back to him, and listened for a response! The sound was echoing up from beneath the very ground I had knelt down on and it frightened me badly. Rising to my feet, I jumped off the spot and began to examine the area further for breaks in the ground that would help me confirm my suspicions. He begin to say I can hear you and feel the pressure of you standing on the ground above and it is making it hard for me to breathe! Suddenly, it was clear to me that he had been beneath the ground for days and needed help! How could I help him, should I run for help or stay and help him? First I needed to mark the spot were I thought he was buried!

He said don't leave me, and I told him that I would be back and he said that someone else told him the same thing two days ago and never came back.

Buried Alive continued

He said again "Help Me" "Help Me, Now"! I had no tools to dig with but my hands; kneeling again, I began to dig with my hands and my nails hoping he would not give up hope. In addition, hoping someone else would pass by to help me dig or go for help while I kept digging and giving him assurance that I had not left him alone!

Amazingly, he was about 3 feet beneath the surface and as I scratched through the moist soil after breaking the surface of the grass, his right hand popped up and grabbed my hand! Oh my God, did that startle me! A hand reaching from beneath the moist earth quickly grabbed my hand clinging to it for dear life. Thoughts ran through my head - what if he is dangerous or what if this is somebody's idea of a cruel hoax! Surely not, but how did he get there -- no time to ask those questions! We were almost to the point where he could begin helping me free him and then he sneezed as we moved the dirt from his face! He began to panic because he could not see, I told him to calm down because there was still dirt on his face and as soon as we remove the dirt, he would be able to see! We moved the dirt from his face and his ears, his eyes, his mouth, and he still could not see! He began to panic again and thought he had lost his sight from being beneath the earth and people walking on top of him must have placed pressure on his eyes!

No time I said to him to figure it out because we had to free the rest of him from this place they had buried him alive. He dug around his body with the strength he had and finally he could free his legs. Reaching for his other hand to pull him up we both struggled and finally he freed from the grave of darkness! He looked at me and I could scarcely make him out beneath the mud on his body. He looked at me and said thank you! As I tried to clean his face some more, this young male voice was an adolescent child peering out from behind that dirt! Before moving him anymore, I asked where he was hurting and if he could walk. He said he was very much in pain from being in that space and from the bad physical beating and left for dead! Those who had done this buried him thinking he was dead, because the last thing during the beating he remembered was losing consciousness. He had no idea of the time he had spent buried or the day it was, and wanted to flee to safety! He told me that the people who had done this to him would not be happy to know he was not dead! How could I hide an adolescent boy without involving the authorities? Maybe his injuries are internal, maybe he has irreparable harm psychologically and not to mention physical

Buried Alive conclusion

impairments that may arise! What am I suppose to do with the child that dead and is now alive? This day that I walked into the Botanical Gardens to enjoy the beauty of the surroundings had turned into a day of redemption for a young child who thought no one would hear his cries for help! We turn the story to you and ask you today; is that young child you? Who left you for dead and crying for help and you think no one hears your cries? Do you think that those who harmed you will stop at nothing to make sure you are dead? If they only had known you, were stronger than they expected and that you would survive the beating and the burial! Could it be that today is the day you get up from the place where they buried you thinking that your story was over? Where did they bury you alive? Is there a way to recover after you have been buried alive by your abusers? My fellow grave partner, the answer is a relationship with Jesus Christ that goes beyond mere words of accepting salvation! This gift of salvation is freely yours, but it is the relationship that requires getting to know the one who has saved you and discovering that he has a plan for your life's' story that exceeds your pain! I invite you hear my testimony of resurrection as one who was left for dead and buried alive by her abusers! I am Patricia E Adams, Author of the One Heart Series an Inductive Study on Intimacy with God. This is how the lover of my soul taught me how to overcome the deadly blows that assaulted my body, my spirit, my mind, my soul, my will and my emotions so thoroughly that there should have only been ashes left! Let us take the Journey of Intimacy with God as from faith to faith and victory through victory in the five volume series entitled "One Heart".

Sincerely One Who Was Dead,
Patricia E Adams,

Touching the Taboo

Taboo defined as an adjective, forbidden or disapproved of; placed under a social prohibition or ban (in Polynesia and other islands of the South Pacific) marked off as simultaneously sacred and forbidden; a noun, any prohibition resulting from social or other conventions; ritual restriction or prohibition, especially of something that is considered holy or unclean; a verb, to place under a taboo. What comes to your mind when you think of things that are harmful to yourself and others? What aftershocks have you experienced because of harmful things done to yourself by yourself or others?

This year we must see this as a new dawn to "RISE" out of and above the shackles that keep us bound. These shackles are on and in the imagery of our mind! As a part of mankind we are perpetually changing. The laws of natural selection operate with or without our cooperation! Thus, change is inevitable and your obligation to participate in the process. This requires a conscious choice to remain fixed or to become fluid and pour and repour you into the next vessel, vehicle and shift that is presented. We must free our minds through spiritual intimacy with God! Intimacy that praises, worships and magnifies one that is greater than the created and collective body of folk. We fail to learn when we worship ourselves; through God we gain wisdom and knowledge which converts to understanding! Above all get an understanding we are told!

 Understanding that is amassed from teaching, correction, and guidance into all Truth! God is the only one who can permanently replace the bitterness that becomes like mildew on the grout between the tiles of our life's' story! Whatever has been done to you and by you that fits under the confines of taboo in your cultural reference point will ultimately be the chains of bondage on your mind! We need a sweet savor to enter our senses through every means of recovering of sight, because we are blinded by who we are to become often by what has been done against us and by us! In comes forgiveness of self and others like a dashing king on a white stallion with red roses braided into its' mane, with a scent of rose on his coat. Love has found its' way back to you seated on the back of this magnificent animal! The King invites you to the Palace, but will you come in his presence wearing mildewed garments or will you dip your garments in the blood of the Lamb that removes the mildew and restores the garment to its' original grandness!

When you make that decision the room fills with a familiar fragrance that is sweet to the senses and enlightens the heart with the sweet savor of love divine! To experience this love divine one must forgive as they have been forgiven, to forgive is divine, and to be divine is to be God-like. When we forgive we are being as God would have us to be, he has forgiven us of much and to hold unforgiveness as if it is your birth right is far from divine! Change is all around us ~ we must change to walk in newness of life, to have a new heart, new mind and new spirit, all require change! How long will we stand halted between two opinions? Either you love God with all of you or you remain as one who sees the relationship of intimacy with God as an observer! This year let's rejoice in the divine nature of God! Kirk Franklin sings a song that Declares: "This Is It" & Imagine Me, which are both songs that speak to a decision made to no longer stand halted between two opinions! The taboos are the things that have been done to you and by you that make you feel unworthily and diminished! It is time for your red carpet debut into all that you were designed to be in the presence of God our King! Only what you do for Christ will last!

Sincerely One Who Was Tabooed,
Patricia E Adams

The Pages of My Life

As Stated in Jeremiah 29:11 God Knew The Thoughts He Was Thinking About Me - Even When I Was Unaware, and they were not thought to harm me, but to keep me as only he was able to do in the midst of the storms of my life. For this reason the pages of my life are filled with the providence of God and it is with this purpose the One Heart Series was birthed!

From the ravages of Satan's' pillaging in my life came a call from God to come away and learn of Him! This series came forth as a result of that journey began over a period of decades in my life, to point others out of your own abyss by sharing topics that were strategic milestones in my life. It is not meant to be a substitute for your religious leader, or professional counselors, but a fellow-companion shining light on your journey to wholeness. For this reason we emphasize that you study to show yourself approved unto God, a workman that needeth not be ashamed, but rightfully dividing the word of truth. (paraphrase of II Timothy 2:15) God set me free from, the post-trauma created by rape, abortion, sexual, physical, emotional, and religious abuse. The first step for me was making a quality decision to no longer remain a victim, a self-imposed prisoner; bound by the chains of the actions of others and wallowing in self-pity. The cycle of abuse endured from the age of 4 years to 30 years of age. During that time, God held the broken pieces of me together as the cycle of abuse others imposed on me seemed would destroy me. But in the midst of Euryclodon (the whirlwind) God said, not so! My first encounter with God came at the age of 9, and it was in the family restroom and in a dream that same night. I now know that God planted a seed that day in me, a seed of assurance that he would see me through. It was not until I reached 30 that the revelation of that night began to unfold in me. Between the years of 18 and 30, I wavered in and out (backslid) from my Lord many times. One morning I arose no longer able to bear the darkness, and the war within my soul. Finally, the prisoner within and reached out. I had become a self-imposed prisoner in a cell without a lock. You see, God had given me permission to go free, and told me that he had made a way of escape. But, I preferred my-self imposed cell over freedom, it was familiar, it was safe so I thought...

OPENING PRAYER:
ALMIGHTY GOD, Thou maker of the land and sea, the hills and valleys, the trees and the flowers, help us to find Thee in Thy world, as well as in Thy Word, and to hear Thee speaking in all about us. Make our thoughts as pure as Thy crystal springs; make our hearts as radiant as Thy sunshine; cultivate our lives till they be as fruitful as Thy orchards. Help us through summer days of pleasure and new scenes never to forget Thee, the Giver of all good and the Saviour of our souls. Take us safely along the journey of life to a new understanding of Thy redeeming love, a new fellowship with Thy Son, a new dedication to Thy service. And Lord, be though within me, to strengthen me; without me, to keep me; above me, to protect me; beneath me, to uphold me; before me, to direct me; behind me, to keep me from straying; round about me, to defend me. Blessed be Thou, our Father, for ever and ever in Jesus Christ Name. Amen

I will instruct thee and teach thee in the way which thou shall go; I will guide thee with mine eye. Psalm 32:8
Create in me a clean heart, O God; and renew a right spirit within me. Psalm 51:10

DAILY

Put on the Whole Armour as a Lifestyle!

Helmet of Salvation
to keep my thoughts aligned with your will

Loins Girt with Truth
to keep me in integrity

Breastplate of Righteousness protect my standing in the community

Gospel of Peace
to order my steps correctly

Shield of Faith
to secure my purpose and destiny

Sword of the Spirit
to reign, rule and have dominion

WEEK One

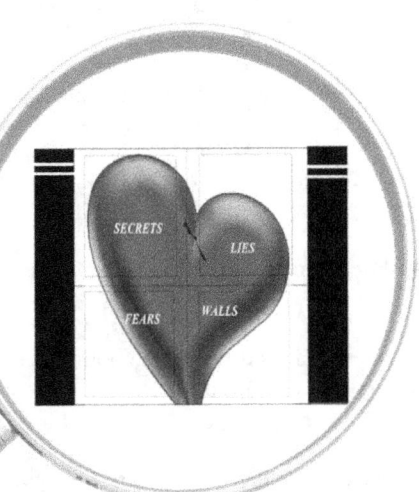

CALENDAR

Day	 	Sat	Sun	Mon	Tue	Wed	Thu	Fri
Date	**Hour**							
1st Watch	6–9 pm							
2nd Watch	9-12 am							
3rd Watch	12–3 am							
4th Watch	3–6 am							
5th Watch	6–9 am							
6th Watch	9–12 pm							
7th Watch	12–3 pm							
8th Watch	3–6 pm							

"Our Master's field is full and rich.
The precious promises lie in front of you.
Gather them.
Make them your own.
Grasp these sweet promises.
Thresh them by meditation.
Feed on them with joy"
C H Spurgeon

Weekly Plan Synopsis *(See Appendix for full plan)*

Day 1
Telling yourself and God the truth about where you are in your heart today! Repent and commit it to God.

Day 2
Pray Psalms 51 in the first person tense for yourself, no matter who has hurt or betrayed you.

Day 3
Continue as an action of intent to forgive. Forgiveness is not a feeling -- but a commandment (to do). Release yourself from the torment, you deserve it. Pray "By faith (trust in God's ability) I choose to forgive those who have caused me pain in Jesus Name. I forgive name them as an act of faith.

Day 4
Begin thanking God for restoring your peace and for his forgiveness because you held onto unforgiveness in your heart!

Day 5
Wherefore my dearly beloved, flee from idolatry. (I Corinthians 10:13-14) Anything that occupies the space in our heart that belongs to God is idolatry.

Day 6
Could you be the one to share the gospel with them and save them from a burning hell! Remember one plants, another waters, and God gives the increase!

Day 7
What fruit can you pick from the Tree of Life to feed your heart today get started feeding the scriptures to your heart to manifest that fruit.

Week One: Broken Heart
Reference: Weekly Plan Outline (See Appendix)

What is a Broken Heart & Spirit and a Contrite Heart?
"The sacrifices of God are a broken spirit: a broken and a contrite heart, O God, thou wilt not despise. " Psalms 51:17 KJV

Two sacrifices that are acceptable to God always are a broken spirit and a contrite heart. In Hebrew the word Shabar means broken, which means to shiver, break in pieces, reduce to splinters bring to the birth, crush and destroy. How can we interpret this passage let's look at it this way: The sacrifices of God are a broken spirit – that is a shivering, splintered, crushed, self-denied place where God can birth himself: and a contrite (dechal) means reduced to powder and (dakah) collapsed and wounded spirit that is in its simplest form ready for the water of the word to create and fulfill God's purpose. You have come to the end of yourself and your desires and are in a surrendered state of being! God promises to hear the broken, save them, have mercy on them, deliver them from fear, deliver out of all troubles, uphold them, reward them, be a refuge for them, remember their weakness, hide them, consider them and give them grace. Because of his faithfulness we can trust Him because He is our King and our Commander of deliverance who will push down our enemies. He will stand against those who stand against us! Thus we totally trust in him and not our abilities. There is no record of Him ever failing! History records how He shamed those who hated us, and we can make our boast in Him forever. He rains on the just as well as the unjust to prove to them that God provides for all creation in spite of their rebellion. But with a promise that if we continue to rebel there is a judgment. The purpose of such goodness to the unsaved is to lead them to repentance (Romans 2:4)

Why would God continue to love us even when we are unloving towards Him? Because of His divine providence! The word providence means foresight and forethought; the care of God over His creatures. His divine superintendence or direction over what He has created. Foresight and forethought on the part of anybody implies intention; God intends our future end to be good and attainable.

Week One: Broken Heart

All of the promises of God reveal that he has provided for man here and now are indicative that the power of curse is broken. Most of our minds are curse conscious until we surrender our lives to the fullness of Gods' benefits. What is besetting you that you can not be broken?

Take Comfort in the following passage(s):

"The LORD is nigh unto them that are of a broken heart; and saveth such as be as of a contrite spirit. Psalms 34:18 KJV

Notes: _____

_____

_____

_____

YOUR PERSONAL COMMITMENT TO GOD

Thanksgiving – Praise – Worship Your Way into His Presence
Opening Prayer (Remember Put on Your Armour!)
Scripture(s) Reading

Call to Action for the Day
Will I chose to believe the truth I've discovered?
Will I allow the truth to change my thinking and my conduct?
We must adjust ourselves to the Bible— never the Bible to ourselves.
Closing Prayer

Week One: Broken Heart

GODS COMMITMENT TO YOU

Promises from the Father _____

_____

Priorities of the Day_____

_____

Benefits for the Day_____

_____

DECLARATIONS AND DECREES

Days Protection_____

_____

_____

_____

Days Strategies _____

_____

_____

_____

Week One: Broken Heart
PRAISE REPORT

Cool of the Day Revelation_____

WEEK Two

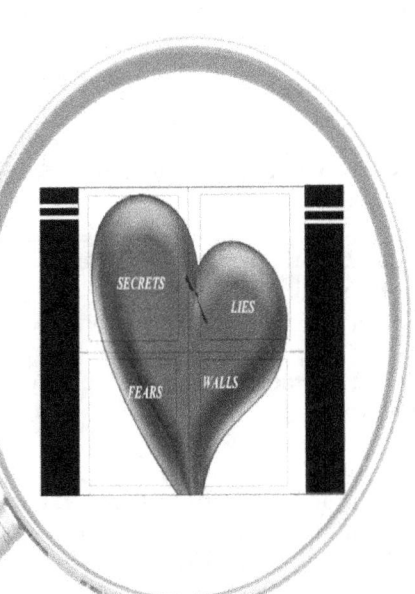

CALENDAR

Day		Sat	Sun	Mon	Tue	Wed	Thu	Fri
Date	Hour							
1st Watch	6–9 pm							
2nd Watch	9–12 am							
3rd Watch	12–3 am							
4th Watch	3–6 am							
5th Watch	6–9 am							
6th Watch	9–12 pm							
7th Watch	12–3 pm							
8th Watch	3–6 pm							

"...The third thing I noticed was a bee, just a little bee. But the bee would light on a flower and it would sink down deep into the flower and it would extract all the nectar and pollen that it could carry. It went in empty every time and came out full"
Naismith, 1200 Notes,
Quotes and Anecdotes
[Chicago: Moody, 1962], p. 15.)

Weekly Plan Synopsis *(See Appendix for full plan)*

Day 1
Telling yourself and God the truth about where you are in your heart today! Repent and commit it to God.

Day 2
Pray Psalms 51 in the first person tense for yourself, no matter who has hurt or betrayed you.

Day 3
Continue as an action of intent to forgive. Forgiveness is not a feeling -- but a commandment (to do). Release yourself from the torment, you deserve it. Pray "By faith (trust in God's ability) I choose to forgive those who have caused me pain in Jesus Name. I forgive name them as an act of faith.

Day 4
Begin thanking God for restoring your peace and for his forgiveness because you held onto unforgiveness in your heart!

Day 5
Wherefore my dearly beloved, flee from idolatry. (I Corinthians 10:13-14) Anything that occupies the space in our heart that belongs to God is idolatry.

Day 6
Could you be the one to share the gospel with them and save them from a burning hell! Remember one plants, another waters, and God gives the increase!

Day 7
What fruit can you pick from the Tree of Life to feed your heart today get started feeding the scriptures to your heart to manifest that fruit.

Week Two: Heart of Wax

Reference: Weekly Plan Outline (See Appendix)

Every day tell yourself the truth, face that truth no matter how ugly it is, repent of it and commit it to God. This is an action not a feeling; you do it by faith continuously until you feel the release in your spirit or until it is no longer a chore but a pleasure!

What is a Heart of Wax?

A heart that is overwhelmed

Christ heart became wax on the Cross as foretold in:
Psalm 22:14 "I am poured out like water, and all my bones are out of joint: my heart is like wax; it is melted in the midst of my bowels." KJV

Psalm 22:14 "I am poured out like {h} water, and all my bones are out of joint: my heart is like wax; it is melted in the midst of my bowels." Geneva Study Bible

The Geneva Study Bible further says regarding this passage that "Before he spoke of the cruelty of his enemies, and now he declares the inward grief of the mind, so that Christ was tormented both in soul and body."

Matthew Henry's Concise Commentary says of Psalm 22:11-21 "In these verses we have Christ suffering, and Christ praying; by which we are directed to look for crosses, and to look up to God under them. The very manner of Christ's death is described...They pierced his hands and his feet, which were nailed to the accursed tree, and his whole body was left so to hang as to suffer the most severe pain and torture. His natural force failed, being wasted by the fire of Divine wrath preying upon his spirits. Who then can stand before God's anger? or who knows the power of it? The life of the sinner was forfeited, and the life

Week Two: Heart of Wax

of the Sacrifice must be the ransom for it. Our Lord Jesus was stripped, when he was crucified, that he might clothe us with the robe of his righteousness....it behoved Christ to suffer. Let all this confirm our faith in him as the true Messiah, and excite our love to him as the best of friends, who loved us, and suffered all this for us. Christ in his agony prayed, prayed earnestly, prayed that the cup might pass from him. When we cannot rejoice in God as our song, yet let us stay ourselves upon him as our strength; and take the comfort of spiritual supports, when we cannot have spiritual delights. He prays to be delivered from the Divine wrath. He that has delivered, doth deliver, and will do so... think upon the sufferings and resurrection of Christ, till we feel in our souls the power of his resurrection, and the fellowship of his sufferings."

Take comfort in the following passage(s):
Psalm 73:26
My flesh and my heart may fail; But God is the strength of my heart and my portion forever. Your portion is to praise, glorify, and fear God because He has heard the cry of the afflicted.

What Weights and Burdens Come to Mind to Lay Down?

_____

_____

YOUR PERSONAL COMMITMENT TO GOD

Thanksgiving – Praise – Worship Your Way into His Presence
Opening Prayer (**Remember Put on Your Armour!**)
Scripture(s) Reading

Call to Action for the Day
Will I chose to believe the truth I've discovered?
Will I allow the truth to change my thinking and my conduct?
We must adjust ourselves to the Bible— never the Bible to ourselves.
Closing Prayer

Week Two: Heart of Wax

GODS COMMITMENT TO YOU

Promises from the Father _____
_____

Priorities of the Day_____
_____

Benefits for the Day_____
_____

DECLARATIONS AND DECREES

Protection_____
_____

Strategies for the Day_____
_____

Week Two: Heart of Wax
PRAISE REPORT

Cool of the Day Revelation_____

_____

_____

_____

_____

_____

_____

_____

_____

_____

_____

WEEK Three

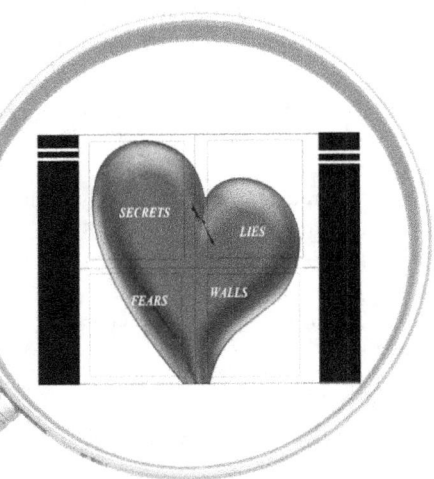

CALENDAR

Day		Sat	Sun	Mon	Tue	Wed	Thu	Fri
Date	**Hour**							
1st Watch	6–9 pm							
2nd Watch	9–12 am							
3rd Watch	12–3 am							
4th Watch	3–6 am							
5th Watch	6–9 am							
6th Watch	9–12 pm							
7th Watch	12–3 pm							
8th Watch	3–6 pm							

"...What a terrible delusion to be content with, to delight in hearing the word, and yet not do it. And how prevalent the sight of multitudes of Christians listening to the Word of God most regularly and earnestly, and yet not doing it!..."
Andrew Murray

Weekly Plan Synopsis *(See Appendix for full plan)*

Day 1
Telling yourself and God the truth about where you are in your heart today! Repent and commit it to God.

Day 2
Pray Psalms 51 in the first person tense for yourself, no matter who has hurt or betrayed you.

Day 3
Continue as an action of intent to forgive. Forgiveness is not a feeling -- but a commandment (to do). Release yourself from the torment, you deserve it. Pray "By faith (trust in God's ability) I choose to forgive those who have caused me pain in Jesus Name. I forgive name them as an act of faith.

Day 4
Begin thanking God for restoring your peace and for his forgiveness because you held onto unforgiveness in your heart!

Day 5
Wherefore my dearly beloved, flee from idolatry. (I Corinthians 10:13-14) Anything that occupies the space in our heart that belongs to God is idolatry.

Day 6
Could you be the one to share the gospel with them and save them from a burning hell! Remember one plants, another waters, and God gives the increase!

Day 7
What fruit can you pick from the Tree of Life to feed your heart today get started feeding the scriptures to your heart to manifest that fruit.

Week Three: Grieved Heart

Reference: Weekly Plan Outline (See Appendix)

Every day tell yourself the truth, face that truth no matter how ugly it is, repent of it and commit it to God. This is an action not a feeling; you do it by faith continuously until you feel the release in your spirit or until it is no longer a chore but a pleasure!

What is a Grieved Heart?
to faint, be depressed and almost overwhelmed with sorrow or burden of mind, to groan and murmur.

Greek
ademoneo Vines Expository Dictionary
"...troubled, much distressed," of the Lord's sorrow in Gethsemane, "to be sore troubled;" of Epaphroditus, because the saints at Philippi had received news of his sickness. A burdened and heavy heart due to Satan's yoke of oppression and of being overworked. What is being presented is hard to be borne up under.

Hebrew
atsab As in God's grief over making man:
1) to hurt, pain, grieve, displease, vex, wrest

God's heart was grieved:
Gen 6:6 (KJV) 6 And it repented the LORD that he had made man on the earth, and it grieved him at his heart.

Heb 3:17-19 (KJV) But with whom was he grieved forty years? was it not with them that had sinned, whose carcasses fell in the wilderness? 18 And to whom sware he that they should not enter into his rest, but to them that believed not? 19 So we see that they could not enter in because of unbelief.

Our hearts when grieved are identified with by Jesus' through his own suffering Matthew 26:36-39 (KJV)

Week Three: Grieved Heart

Take comfort in the following passage:
Isaiah 53:4-5 KJV
But he was wounded for our transgressions, he was bruised for our iniquities: the chastisement of our peace was upon him; and with his stripes we are healed.

He took our discipline, chastening, correction so that we would have completeness (in number), b) safety, soundness (in body), c) welfare, health, prosperity, d) peace, quiet, tranquility, contentment, e) peace, friendship 1) of human relationships 2) with God especially in covenant relationship f) peace (from war) g) peace (as adjective)
Source: Blue Letter Bible

What Weights and Burdens Come to Mind to Lay Down?

_____

_____

YOUR PERSONAL COMMITMENT TO GOD

Thanksgiving – Praise – Worship Your Way into His Presence
Opening Prayer (Remember Put on Your Armour!)
Scripture(s) Reading

Call to Action for the Day
Will I chose to believe the truth I've discovered?
Will I allow the truth to change my thinking and my conduct?
We must adjust ourselves to the Bible— never the Bible to ourselves.
Closing Prayer

Week Three: Grieved Heart

GODS COMMITMENT TO YOU

Promises from the Father _____

_____

Priorities of the Day_____

_____

Benefits for the Day_____

_____

DECLARATIONS AND DECREES

Protection_____

_____

Strategies for the Day_____

_____

Week Three: Grieved Heart
PRAISE REPORT

Cool of the Day Revelation_____

WEEK Four

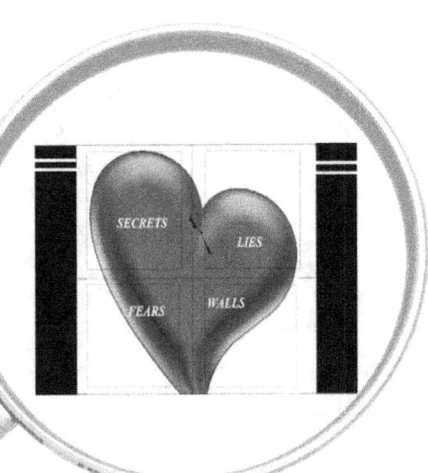

CALENDAR

Day	♥	Sat	Sun	Mon	Tue	Wed	Thu	Fri
Date	Hour							
1st Watch	6–9 pm							
2nd Watch	9–12 am							
3rd Watch	12–3 am							
4th Watch	3–6 am							
5th Watch	6–9 am							
6th Watch	9–12 pm							
7th Watch	12–3 pm							
8th Watch	3–6 pm							

"...It is not enough just to study the Bible. We must meditate upon it. In a very real sense we are giving our brain a bath; we are washing it in the purifying solution of God's Word...."

(cp note Ephesians 5:26).
(MacArthur, J.:
The MacArthur Study Bible Nashville: Word or Logos)

Weekly Plan Synopsis *(See Appendix for full plan)*
Day 1
Telling yourself and God the truth about where you are in your heart today! Repent and commit it to God.

Day 2
Pray Psalms 51 in the first person tense for yourself, no matter who has hurt or betrayed you.

Day 3
Continue as an action of intent to forgive. Forgiveness is not a feeling -- but a commandment (to do). Release yourself from the torment, you deserve it. Pray "By faith (trust in God's ability) I choose to forgive those who have caused me pain in Jesus Name. I forgive name them as an act of faith.

Day 4
Begin thanking God for restoring your peace and for his forgiveness because you held onto unforgiveness in your heart!

Day 5
Wherefore my dearly beloved, flee from idolatry. (I Corinthians 10:13-14) Anything that occupies the space in our heart that belongs to God is idolatry.

Day 6
Could you be the one to share the gospel with them and save them from a burning hell! Remember one plants, another waters, and God gives the increase!

Day 7
What fruit can you pick from the Tree of Life to feed your heart today get started feeding the scriptures to your heart to manifest that fruit.

Week Four: Willing Heart

Reference: Weekly Plan Outline (See Appendix)
Every day tell yourself the truth, face that truth no matter how ugly it is, repent of it and commit it to God. This is an action not a feeling; you do it by faith continuously until you feel the release in your spirit or until it is no longer a chore but a pleasure!

What is a Willing Heart?

Hebrew: leb
1) inner man, mind, will, heart, understanding
a) inner part, midst
1) midst (of things)
2) heart (of man)
3) soul, heart (of man)
4) mind, knowledge, thinking, reflection, memory
5) inclination, resolution, determination (of will)
6) conscience
7) heart (of moral character)
8) as seat of appetites
9) as seat of emotions and passions
10) as seat of courage

Hebrew: nadiyb
1) inclined, willing, noble, generous
a) incited, inclined, willing
b) noble, princely (in rank)
c) noble (in mind and character)

Remember Jesus has proven himself faithful so that engrafted and adopted sons would receive the anointing to be faithful through his obedience to the Father.

Week Four: Willing Heart

Take comfort in the following passage:
Exodus 35:5 (KJV)
5 Take ye from among you an offering unto the LORD: whosoever is of a willing heart, let him bring it, an offering of the LORD; gold, and silver, and brass,

2 Corinthians 8:11 (KJV)
11 Now therefore perform the doing of it; that as there was a readiness to will, so there may be a performance also out of that which ye have.

What Weights and Burdens Come to Mind to Lay Down?

_____

_____

YOUR PERSONAL COMMITMENT TO GOD

Thanksgiving – Praise – Worship Your Way into His Presence
Opening Prayer (Remember Put on Your Armour!)
Scripture(s) Reading

Call to Action for the Day
Will I chose to believe the truth I've discovered?
Will I allow the truth to change my thinking and my conduct?
We must adjust ourselves to the Bible— never the Bible to ourselves.
Closing Prayer

Week Four: Willing Heart

GODS COMMITMENT TO YOU

Promises from the Father _____

_____

Priorities of the Day_____

_____

Benefits for the Day_____

_____

DECLARATIONS AND DECREES

Protection_____

_____

Strategies for the Day_____

_____

Week Four: Willing Heart
PRAISE REPORT

Cool of the Day Revelation_____

WEEK Five

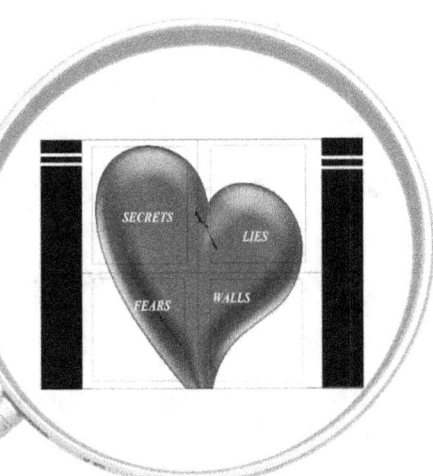

CALENDAR

Day	♥	Sat	Sun	Mon	Tue	Wed	Thu	Fri
Date	Hour							
1st Watch	6–9 pm							
2nd Watch	9–12 am							
3rd Watch	12–3 am							
4th Watch	3–6 am							
5th Watch	6–9 am							
6th Watch	9–12 pm							
7th Watch	12–3 pm							
8th Watch	3–6 pm							

"...There is more to Christian growth than knowing what the Bible says; nobody is ever nourished by memorizing menus..."
John Blanchard

Weekly Plan Synopsis *(See Appendix for full plan)*

Day 1
Telling yourself and God the truth about where you are in your heart today! Repent and commit it to God.

Day 2
Pray Psalms 51 in the first person tense for yourself, no matter who has hurt or betrayed you.

Day 3
Continue as an action of intent to forgive. Forgiveness is not a feeling -- but a commandment (to do). Release yourself from the torment, you deserve it. Pray "By faith (trust in God's ability) I choose to forgive those who have caused me pain in Jesus Name. I forgive name them as an act of faith.

Day 4
Begin thanking God for restoring your peace and for his forgiveness because you held onto unforgiveness in your heart!

Day 5
Wherefore my dearly beloved, flee from idolatry. (I Corinthians 10:13-14) Anything that occupies the space in our heart that belongs to God is idolatry.

Day 6
Could you be the one to share the gospel with them and save them from a burning hell! Remember one plants, another waters, and God gives the increase!

Day 7
What fruit can you pick from the Tree of Life to feed your heart today get started feeding the scriptures to your heart to manifest that fruit.

Week Five: Faithful Heart

Reference: Weekly Plan Outline (See Appendix)

Every day tell yourself the truth, face that truth no matter how ugly it is, repent of it and commit it to God. This is an action not a feeling; you do it by faith continuously until you feel the release in your spirit or until it is no longer a chore but a pleasure!

What is a Faithful Heart?

Greek pistov pistos pis-tos'
1) trusty, faithful
1a) of persons who show themselves faithful in the transaction of business, the execution of commands, or the discharge of official duties
1b) one who kept his plighted faith, worthy of trust
1c) that can be relied on
2) easily persuaded
2a) believing, confiding, trusting
2b) in the NT one who trusts in God's promises
2b1) one who is convinced that Jesus has been raised from the dead
2b2) one who has become convinced that Jesus is the Messiah and author of salvation

Hebrew 'aman aw-man'
1a1) to support, confirm, be faithful, uphold, nourish
1a1a) foster-father (subst.)
1a1b) foster-mother, nurse
1a1c) pillars, supporters of the door

Week Five: Faithful Heart

Take comfort in the following passage(s):

Matthew 24:45 Who then is a faithful and wise servant, whom his lord hath made ruler over his household, to give them meat in due season?

Matthew 25:21 His lord said unto him, Well done, thou good and faithful servant: thou hast been faithful over a few things, I will make thee ruler over many things: enter thou into the joy of thy lord.

Genesis 15:6 And he believed in the LORD; and he counted it to him for righteousness. Remember Jesus has proven himself faithful so that engrafted and adopted sons would receive the anointing to be faithful through his obedience to the Father.

What Weights and Burdens Come to Mind to Lay Down?

_____

_____

YOUR PERSONAL COMMITMENT TO GOD

Thanksgiving – Praise – Worship Your Way into His Presence
Opening Prayer (Remember Put on Your Armour!)
Scripture(s) Reading

Call to Action for the Day
Will I chose to believe the truth I've discovered?
Will I allow the truth to change my thinking and my conduct?
We must adjust ourselves to the Bible— never the Bible to ourselves.
Closing Prayer

Week Five: Faithful Heart

GODS COMMITMENT TO YOU

Promises from the Father _____

_____

Priorities of the Day_____

_____

Benefits for the Day_____

_____

DECLARATIONS AND DECREES

Protection_____

_____

Strategies for the Day_____

_____

Week Five: Faithful Heart
PRAISE REPORT

Cool of the Day Revelation_____

_____

_____

_____

_____

_____

_____

_____

_____

_____

_____

_____

WEEK Six

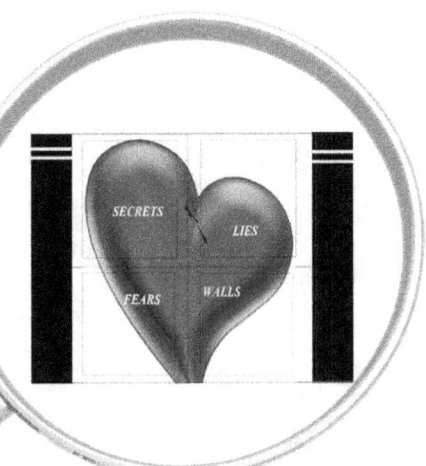

CALENDAR

Day		Sat	Sun	Mon	Tue	Wed	Thu	Fri
Date	Hour							
1st Watch	6–9 pm							
2nd Watch	9–12 am							
3rd Watch	12–3 am							
4th Watch	3–6 am							
5th Watch	6–9 am							
6th Watch	9–12 pm							
7th Watch	12–3 pm							
8th Watch	3–6 pm							

Lay hold on the Bible until the Bible lays hold on you.
Will H. Houghton

Weekly Plan Synopsis *(See Appendix for full plan)*

Day 1
Telling yourself and God the truth about where you are in your heart today! Repent and commit it to God.

Day 2
Pray Psalms 51 in the first person tense for yourself, no matter who has hurt or betrayed you.

Day 3
Continue as an action of intent to forgive. Forgiveness is not a feeling -- but a commandment (to do). Release yourself from the torment, you deserve it. Pray "By faith (trust in God's ability) I choose to forgive those who have caused me pain in Jesus Name. I forgive name them as an act of faith.

Day 4
Begin thanking God for restoring your peace and for his forgiveness because you held onto unforgiveness in your heart!

Day 5
Wherefore my dearly beloved, flee from idolatry. (I Corinthians 10:13-14) Anything that occupies the space in our heart that belongs to God is idolatry.

Day 6
Could you be the one to share the gospel with them and save them from a burning hell! Remember one plants, another waters, and God gives the increase!

Day 7
What fruit can you pick from the Tree of Life to feed your heart today get started feeding the scriptures to your heart to manifest that fruit.

Week Six: Communing and Sound Heart

Reference: Weekly Plan Outline (See Appendix)
Every day tell yourself the truth, face that truth no matter how ugly it is, repent of it and commit it to God. This is an action not a feeling; you do it by faith continuously until you feel the release in your spirit or until it is no longer a chore but a pleasure!

What is a Sound Heart?
Having perfect soundness, wholeness and integrity – which is congruency: where your actions line up with your words.

"A sound heart is the life of the flesh: but envy is the rottenness of the bones." Proverbs 14:30

"Medical science has come to understand that there is a strong relationship between a person's mental and physical health."
http://www.atenizo.org/bible-science.htm

"The light of the eyes rejoices the heart: and a good report makes the bones fat (health)." Proverbs 15:30
"Pleasant words are as a honeycomb, sweet to the soul, and health to the bones." Proverbs 16:24
"A merry heart does good like a medicine: but a broken spirit dries the bones." Proverbs 17:22

What is a Communing Heart?
A heart that talks to God; confers (value his input), reasons with Him and has an intelligent discourse.

Stand in awe, and sin not: commune with your own heart upon your bed, and be still. Selah. Psalms 4:4 (KJV)

Test yourselves [to see] if you are in the faith. Examine yourselves. Or do you not recognize for yourselves that Jesus Christ is in you?—unless you fail the test. II Corinthians 13:5 (Holman Christian Standard Bible)

Week Six Communing and Sound Heart

Take comfort in the following passage:

6 When, on my bed, I think of You, I meditate on You during the night watches 7 because You are my help; I will rejoice in the shadow of Your wings. 8 I follow close to You; Your right hand holds on to me. Psalms 63:6-8 (HCSB)

What Weights and Burdens Come to Mind to Lay Down?

_____

_____

YOUR PERSONAL COMMITMENT TO GOD

Thanksgiving – Praise – Worship Your Way into His Presence
Opening Prayer (Remember Put on Your Armour!)
Scripture(s) Reading

Call to Action for the Day
Will I chose to believe the truth I've discovered?
Will I allow the truth to change my thinking and my conduct?
We must adjust ourselves to the Bible— never the Bible to ourselves.
Closing Prayer

Week Six: Communing and Sound Heart

GODS COMMITMENT TO YOU

Promises from the Father _____
_____

Priorities of the Day_____
_____

Benefits for the Day_____
_____

DECLARATIONS AND DECREES

Protection_____
_____

Strategies for the Day_____
_____

Week Six: Communing and Sound Heart
PRAISE REPORT

Cool of the Day Revelation_____

_____

_____

_____

_____

_____

_____

_____

_____

_____

_____

_____

_____

WEEK Seven

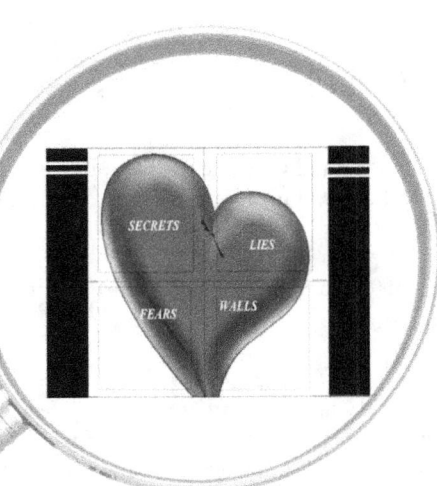

CALENDAR

Day	♥	Sat	Sun	Mon	Tue	Wed	Thu	Fri
Date	Hour							
1st Watch	6–9 pm							
2nd Watch	9-12 am							
3rd Watch	12–3 am							
4th Watch	3–6 am							
5th Watch	6–9 am							
6th Watch	9–12 pm							
7th Watch	12–3 pm							
8th Watch	3–6 pm							

As we search the Scriptures, we must allow them to search us, to sit in judgment upon our character and conduct.
Jerry Bridges

Weekly Plan Synopsis *(See Appendix for full plan)*

Day 1
Telling yourself and God the truth about where you are in your heart today! Repent and commit it to God.

Day 2
Pray Psalms 51 in the first person tense for yourself, no matter who has hurt or betrayed you.

Day 3
Continue as an action of intent to forgive. Forgiveness is not a feeling -- but a commandment (to do). Release yourself from the torment, you deserve it. Pray "By faith (trust in God's ability) I choose to forgive those who have caused me pain in Jesus Name. I forgive name them as an act of faith.

Day 4
Begin thanking God for restoring your peace and for his forgiveness because you held onto unforgiveness in your heart!

Day 5
Wherefore my dearly beloved, flee from idolatry. (I Corinthians 10:13-14) Anything that occupies the space in our heart that belongs to God is idolatry.

Day 6
Could you be the one to share the gospel with them and save them from a burning hell! Remember one plants, another waters, and God gives the increase!

Day 7
What fruit can you pick from the Tree of Life to feed your heart today get started feeding the scriptures to your heart to manifest that fruit.

Week Seven: Proud Heart

Reference: Weekly Plan Outline (See Appendix)
Every day tell yourself the truth, face that truth no matter how ugly it is, repent of it and commit it to God. This is an action not a feeling; you do it by faith continuously until you feel the release in your spirit or until it is no longer a chore but a pleasure!

What is a Proud Heart?

Hebrew: zed
1) arrogant, proud, insolent, presumptuous
a) the arrogant ones
b) presumptuous

Psalm 101:5
Whoso privily slandereth his neighbour him will I cut off: him that hath an high look and a proud heart will not I suffer.

Proverbs 21:4
An high look, and a proud heart, [and] the plowing of the wicked, [is] sin.

Proverbs 28:25
He that is of a proud heart stirreth up strife: but he that putteth his trust in the LORD shall be made fat.

Remember Jesus has proven himself faithful so that engrafted and adopted sons would receive the anointing to be faithful through his obedience to the Father.

Week Seven: Proud Heart

Take comfort in the following passage:
Psalms 119:33-36 (KJV)
33 Teach me, O LORD, the way of thy statutes; and I shall keep it unto the end.
34 Give me understanding, and I shall keep thy law; yea, I shall observe it with my whole heart.
35 Make me to go in the path of thy commandments; for therein do I delight.
36 Incline my heart unto thy testimonies, and not to covetousness.

What Weights and Burdens Come to Mind to Lay Down?

_____

_____

YOUR PERSONAL COMMITMENT TO GOD

Thanksgiving – Praise – Worship Your Way into His Presence
Opening Prayer (Remember Put on Your Armour!)
Scripture(s) Reading

Call to Action for the Day
Will I chose to believe the truth I've discovered?
Will I allow the truth to change my thinking and my conduct?
We must adjust ourselves to the Bible— never the Bible to ourselves.
Closing Prayer

Week Seven: Proud Heart

GODS COMMITMENT TO YOU

Promises from the Father _____

_____

Priorities of the Day_____

_____

Benefits for the Day_____

_____

DECLARATIONS AND DECREES

Protection_____

_____

Strategies for the Day_____

_____

Week Seven: Proud Heart

PRAISE REPORT

Cool of the Day Revelation_____

_____

_____

_____

_____

_____

_____

_____

_____

_____

_____

_____

WEEK Eight

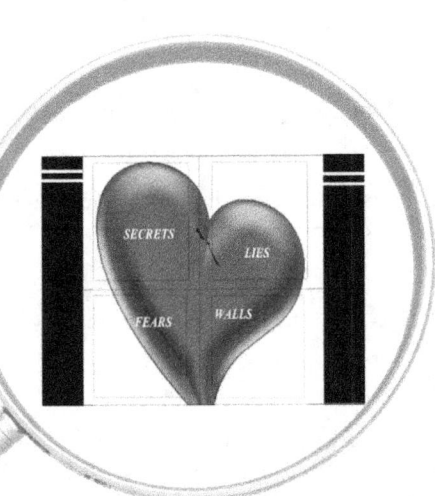

CALENDAR

Day		Sat	Sun	Mon	Tue	Wed	Thu	Fri
Date	Hour							
1st Watch	6–9 pm							
2nd Watch	9–12 am							
3rd Watch	12–3 am							
4th Watch	3–6 am							
5th Watch	6–9 am							
6th Watch	9–12 pm							
7th Watch	12–3 pm							
8th Watch	3–6 pm							

The only Bible the world reads is the one bound in shoe leather:
you and me!
D.L. Moody

Weekly Plan Synopsis *(See Appendix for full plan)*

Day 1
Telling yourself and God the truth about where you are in your heart today! Repent and commit it to God.

Day 2
Pray Psalms 51 in the first person tense for yourself, no matter who has hurt or betrayed you.

Day 3
Continue as an action of intent to forgive. Forgiveness is not a feeling -- but a commandment (to do). Release yourself from the torment, you deserve it. Pray "By faith (trust in God's ability) I choose to forgive those who have caused me pain in Jesus Name. I forgive name them as an act of faith.

Day 4
Begin thanking God for restoring your peace and for his forgiveness because you held onto unforgiveness in your heart!

Day 5
Wherefore my dearly beloved, flee from idolatry. (I Corinthians 10:13-14) Anything that occupies the space in our heart that belongs to God is idolatry.

Day 6
Could you be the one to share the gospel with them and save them from a burning hell! Remember one plants, another waters, and God gives the increase!

Day 7
What fruit can you pick from the Tree of Life to feed your heart today get started feeding the scriptures to your heart to manifest that fruit.

Week Eight: Wicked Heart

Reference: Weekly Plan Outline (See Appendix)

Every day tell yourself the truth, face that truth no matter how ugly it is, repent of it and commit it to God. This is an action not a feeling; you do it by faith continuously until you feel the release in your spirit or until it is no longer a chore but a pleasure!

What is a Wicked Heart?

Hebrew: beliya`al
1) worthlessness
a) worthless, good for nothing, unprofitable, base fellow
b) wicked
c) ruin, destruction (construct)

Hebrew: ra
1) bad, evil
a) bad, disagreeable, malignant
b) bad, unpleasant, evil (giving pain, unhappiness, misery)
c) evil, displeasing

Psalm 101:5
Whoso privily slandereth his neighbour him will I cut off: him that hath an high look and a proud heart will not I suffer.

Proverbs 21:4
An high look, and a proud heart, [and] the plowing of the wicked, [is] sin.

Remember Jesus has proven himself faithful so that engrafted and adopted sons would receive the anointing to be faithful through his obedience to the Father.

Week Eight: Wicked Heart

Take comfort in the following passage:

Proverbs 28:25
He that is of a proud heart stirreth up strife: but he that putteth his trust in the LORD shall be made fat.

Proverbs 10:20-22
20 The tongue of the just is as choice silver: the heart of the wicked is little worth. 21 The lips of the righteous feed many: but fools die for want of wisdom. 22 The blessing of the LORD, it maketh rich, and he addeth no sorrow with it.

Proverbs 15:28-29
28 The heart of the righteous studieth to answer: but the mouth of the wicked poureth out evil things.
29 The LORD is far from the wicked: but he heareth the prayer of the righteous.

What Weights and Burdens Come to Mind to Lay Down?

_____

_____

YOUR PERSONAL COMMITMENT TO GOD

Thanksgiving – Praise – Worship Your Way into His Presence
Opening Prayer (Remember Put on Your Armour!)
Scripture(s) Reading

Call to Action for the Day
Will I chose to believe the truth I've discovered?
Will I allow the truth to change my thinking and my conduct?
We must adjust ourselves to the Bible— never the Bible to ourselves.
Closing Prayer

Week Eight: Wicked Heart

GODS COMMITMENT TO YOU

Promises from the Father _____

_____

Priorities of the Day_____

_____

Benefits for the Day_____

_____

DECLARATIONS AND DECREES

Protection_____

_____

Strategies for the Day_____

_____

Week Eight: Wicked Heart

PRAISE REPORT

Cool of the Day Revelation_____

_____

_____

_____

_____

_____

_____

_____

_____

_____

_____

WEEK Nine

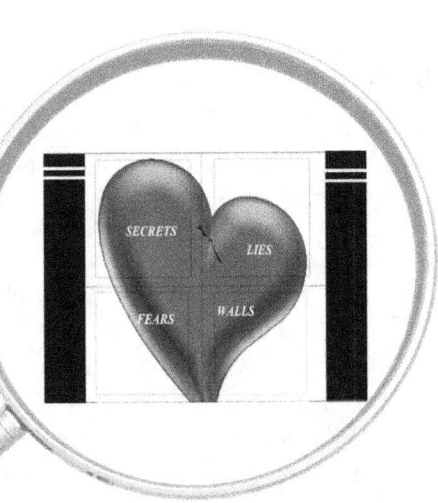

CALENDAR

Day		Sat	Sun	Mon	Tue	Wed	Thu	Fri
Date	Hour							
1st Watch	6–9 pm							
2nd Watch	9-12 am							
3rd Watch	12–3 am							
4th Watch	3–6 am							
5th Watch	6–9 am							
6th Watch	9–12 pm							
7th Watch	12–3 pm							
8th Watch	3–6 pm							

The Word is both a glass to show us the spots of our soul and a laver to wash them away.
Thomas Watson

Weekly Plan Synopsis *(See Appendix for full plan)*

Day 1
Telling yourself and God the truth about where you are in your heart today! Repent and commit it to God.

Day 2
Pray Psalms 51 in the first person tense for yourself, no matter who has hurt or betrayed you.

Day 3
Continue as an action of intent to forgive. Forgiveness is not a feeling -- but a commandment (to do). Release yourself from the torment, you deserve it. Pray "By faith (trust in God's ability) I choose to forgive those who have caused me pain in Jesus Name. I forgive name them as an act of faith.

Day 4
Begin thanking God for restoring your peace and for his forgiveness because you held onto unforgiveness in your heart!

Day 5
Wherefore my dearly beloved, flee from idolatry. (I Corinthians 10:13-14) Anything that occupies the space in our heart that belongs to God is idolatry.

Day 6
Could you be the one to share the gospel with them and save them from a burning hell! Remember one plants, another waters, and God gives the increase!

Day 7
What fruit can you pick from the Tree of Life to feed your heart today get started feeding the scriptures to your heart to manifest that fruit.

Week Nine: Trembling Heart

Reference: Weekly Plan Outline (See Appendix)

Every day tell yourself the truth, face that truth no matter how ugly it is, repent of it and commit it to God. This is an action not a feeling; you do it by faith continuously until you feel the release in your spirit or until it is no longer a chore but a pleasure!

What is a Trembling Heart?
A Heart that fells or expresses fear or anxiety.

Hebrew: raggaz
trembling, quivering, quaking

Greek: tromos
1) a trembling or quaking with fear
2) with fear and trembling, used to describe the anxiety of one who distrusts his ability completely to meet all requirements, but religiously does his utmost to fulfil his duty

Deuteronomy 28:65 And among these nations shalt thou find no ease, neither shall the sole of thy foot have rest: but the LORD shall give thee there a trembling heart, and failing of eyes, and sorrow of mind:

Remember Jesus has proven himself faithful so that engrafted and adopted sons would receive the anointing to be faithful through his obedience to the Father.

Week Nine: Trembling Heart

Take comfort in the following passage:

Ephesians 6:5 Servants, be obedient to them that are [your] masters according to the flesh, with fear and trembling, in singleness of your heart, as unto Christ;

What Weights and Burdens Come to Mind to Lay Down?

_____

_____

YOUR PERSONAL COMMITMENT TO GOD

Thanksgiving – Praise – Worship Your Way into His Presence
Opening Prayer (Remember Put on Your Armour!)
Scripture(s) Reading

Call to Action for the Day
Will I chose to believe the truth I've discovered?
Will I allow the truth to change my thinking and my conduct?
We must adjust ourselves to the Bible— never the Bible to ourselves.
Closing Prayer

Week Nine: Trembling Heart

GODS COMMITMENT TO YOU

Promises from the Father _____

_____

Priorities of the Day_____

_____

Benefits for the Day_____

_____

DECLARATIONS AND DECREES

Protection_____

_____

Strategies for the Day_____

_____

Week Nine: Trembling Heart
PRAISE REPORT

Cool of the Day Revelation_____

WEEK Ten

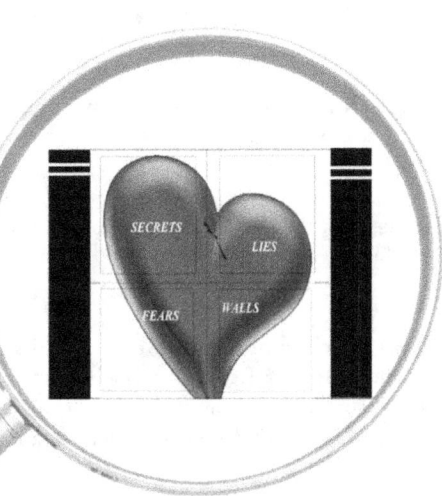

CALENDAR

Day		Sat	Sun	Mon	Tue	Wed	Thu	Fri
Date	Hour							
1st Watch	6–9 pm							
2nd Watch	9–12 am							
3rd Watch	12–3 am							
4th Watch	3–6 am							
5th Watch	6–9 am							
6th Watch	9–12 pm							
7th Watch	12–3 pm							
8th Watch	3–6 pm							

What we take in by the Word we digest by meditation and let out by prayer.
Thomas Manton

Weekly Plan Synopsis *(See Appendix for full plan)*

Day 1
Telling yourself and God the truth about where you are in your heart today! Repent and commit it to God.

Day 2
Pray Psalms 51 in the first person tense for yourself, no matter who has hurt or betrayed you.

Day 3
Continue as an action of intent to forgive. Forgiveness is not a feeling -- but a commandment (to do). Release yourself from the torment, you deserve it. Pray "By faith (trust in God's ability) I choose to forgive those who have caused me pain in Jesus Name. I forgive name them as an act of faith.

Day 4
Begin thanking God for restoring your peace and for his forgiveness because you held onto unforgiveness in your heart!

Day 5
Wherefore my dearly beloved, flee from idolatry. (I Corinthians 10:13-14) Anything that occupies the space in our heart that belongs to God is idolatry.

Day 6
Could you be the one to share the gospel with them and save them from a burning hell! Remember one plants, another waters, and God gives the increase!

Day 7
What fruit can you pick from the Tree of Life to feed your heart today get started feeding the scriptures to your heart to manifest that fruit.

Week Ten: Perfect Heart

Reference: Weekly Plan Outline (See Appendix)

Every day tell yourself the truth, face that truth no matter how ugly it is, repent of it and commit it to God. This is an action not a feeling; you do it by faith continuously until you feel the release in your spirit or until it is no longer a chore but a pleasure!

What is a Perfect Heart?
A Heart lacking in no essentials, it is complete.

Hebrew: shalem shä·lam'
perfect, whole, full, just, peaceable

Greek: teleioo te-la-o'-o
make perfect, perfect, finish, fulfil, be perfect, consecrate

2 Kings 20:3 I beseech thee, O LORD, remember now how I have walked before thee in truth and with a perfect heart, and have done [that which is] good in thy sight. And Hezekiah wept sore.

2 Chronicles 16:9 For the eyes of the LORD run to and fro throughout the whole earth, to shew himself strong in the behalf of [them] whose heart [is] perfect toward him. Herein thou hast done foolishly: therefore from henceforth thou shalt have wars.

Remember Jesus has proven himself faithful so that engrafted and adopted sons would receive the anointing to be faithful through his obedience to the Father.

Week Ten: Perfect Heart

Take comfort in the following passage:

1 Kings 8:61 Let your heart therefore be perfect with the LORD our God, to walk in his statutes, and to keep his commandments, as at this day

What Weights and Burdens Come to Mind to Lay Down?

_____

_____

YOUR PERSONAL COMMITMENT TO GOD

Thanksgiving – Praise – Worship Your Way into His Presence
Opening Prayer (Remember Put on Your Armour!)
Scripture(s) Reading

Call to Action for the Day
Will I chose to believe the truth I've discovered?
Will I allow the truth to change my thinking and my conduct?
We must adjust ourselves to the Bible— never the Bible to ourselves.
Closing Prayer

Week Ten: Perfect Heart

GODS COMMITMENT TO YOU

Promises from the Father _____
_____

Priorities of the Day_____
_____

Benefits for the Day_____
_____

DECLARATIONS AND DECREES

Protection_____
_____

Strategies for the Day_____
_____

Week Ten: Perfect Heart

PRAISE REPORT

Cool of the Day Revelation_____

_____

_____

_____

_____

_____

_____

_____

_____

_____

_____

_____

WEEK Eleven

CALENDAR

Day		Sat	Sun	Mon	Tue	Wed	Thu	Fri
Date	Hour							
1st Watch	6–9 pm							
2nd Watch	9–12 am							
3rd Watch	12–3 am							
4th Watch	3–6 am							
5th Watch	6–9 am							
6th Watch	9–12 pm							
7th Watch	12–3 pm							
8th Watch	3–6 pm							

"In truth thou canst not read the Scriptures too much;..."
Martin Luther

Weekly Plan Synopsis *(See Appendix for full plan)*

Day 1
Telling yourself and God the truth about where you are in your heart today! Repent and commit it to God.

Day 2
Pray Psalms 51 in the first person tense for yourself, no matter who has hurt or betrayed you.

Day 3
Continue as an action of intent to forgive. Forgiveness is not a feeling -- but a commandment (to do). Release yourself from the torment, you deserve it. Pray "By faith (trust in God's ability) I choose to forgive those who have caused me pain in Jesus Name. I forgive name them as an act of faith.

Day 4
Begin thanking God for restoring your peace and for his forgiveness because you held onto unforgiveness in your heart!

Day 5
Wherefore my dearly beloved, flee from idolatry. (I Corinthians 10:13-14) Anything that occupies the space in our heart that belongs to God is idolatry.

Day 6
Could you be the one to share the gospel with them and save them from a burning hell! Remember one plants, another waters, and God gives the increase!

Day 7
What fruit can you pick from the Tree of Life to feed your heart today get started feeding the scriptures to your heart to manifest that fruit.

Week Eleven: Meek Heart

Reference: Weekly Plan Outline (See Appendix)

Every day tell yourself the truth, face that truth no matter how ugly it is, repent of it and commit it to God. This is an action not a feeling; you do it by faith continuously until you feel the release in your spirit or until it is no longer a chore but a pleasure!

What is a Meek Heart?

Hebrew: `anav ä näv'
meek, humble, poor, lowly, vr meek

Greek: praos prä'-os
gentle, mild, meek

Matthew 11:29 Take my yoke upon you, and learn of me; for I am meek and lowly in heart: and ye shall find rest unto your souls.

Remember Jesus has proven himself faithful so that engrafted and adopted sons would receive the anointing to be faithful through his obedience to the Father.

Week Eleven: Meek Heart

Take comfort in the following passage:

Psalms 22:26-28 (KJV)
26 The meek shall eat and be satisfied: they shall praise the LORD that seek him: your heart shall live for ever. 27 All the ends of the world shall remember and turn unto the LORD: and all the kindreds of the nations shall worship before thee. 28 For the kingdom is the LORD'S: and he is the governor among the nations.

What Weights and Burdens Come to Mind to Lay Down?

_____

_____

YOUR PERSONAL COMMITMENT TO GOD

Thanksgiving – Praise – Worship Your Way into His Presence
Opening Prayer (Remember Put on Your Armour!)
Scripture(s) Reading

Call to Action for the Day
Will I chose to believe the truth I've discovered?
Will I allow the truth to change my thinking and my conduct?
We must adjust ourselves to the Bible— never the Bible to ourselves.
Closing Prayer

Week Eleven: Meek Heart

GODS COMMITMENT TO YOU

Promises from the Father _____

_____

Priorities of the Day _____

_____

Benefits for the Day _____

_____

DECLARATIONS AND DECREES

Protection _____

_____

Strategies for the Day _____

_____

Week Eleven: Meek Heart

PRAISE REPORT

Cool of the Day Revelation_____

_____

_____

_____

_____

_____

_____

_____

_____

_____

_____

WEEK Twelve

CALENDAR

Day		Sat	Sun	Mon	Tue	Wed	Thu	Fri
Date	Hour							
1st Watch	6–9 pm							
2nd Watch	9-12 am							
3rd Watch	12–3 am							
4th Watch	3–6 am							
5th Watch	6–9 am							
6th Watch	9–12 pm							
7th Watch	12–3 pm							
8th Watch	3–6 pm							

> *"...And what thou readest, thou canst not read too well;..."*
> Martin Luther

Weekly Plan Synopsis *(See Appendix for full plan)*

Day 1
Telling yourself and God the truth about where you are in your heart today! Repent and commit it to God.

Day 2
Pray Psalms 51 in the first person tense for yourself, no matter who has hurt or betrayed you.

Day 3
Continue as an action of intent to forgive. Forgiveness is not a feeling -- but a commandment (to do). Release yourself from the torment, you deserve it. Pray "By faith (trust in God's ability) I choose to forgive those who have caused me pain in Jesus Name. I forgive name them as an act of faith.

Day 4
Begin thanking God for restoring your peace and for his forgiveness because you held onto unforgiveness in your heart!

Day 5
Wherefore my dearly beloved, flee from idolatry. (I Corinthians 10:13-14) Anything that occupies the space in our heart that belongs to God is idolatry.

Day 6
Could you be the one to share the gospel with them and save them from a burning hell! Remember one plants, another waters, and God gives the increase!

Day 7
What fruit can you pick from the Tree of Life to feed your heart today get started feeding the scriptures to your heart to manifest that fruit.

Week Twelve: Double Heart

Reference: Weekly Plan Outline (See Appendix)

Every day tell yourself the truth, face that truth no matter how ugly it is, repent of it and commit it to God. This is an action not a feeling; you do it by faith continuously until you feel the release in your spirit or until it is no longer a chore but a pleasure!

What is a Double Heart?

A Heart composed of two unlike parts acting in duplicity.

Hebrew: kaphal kä ·fal' double
Greek: dipsychos de'-psü-khos double minded

Psalms 12:2 (KJV)
2 They speak vanity every one with his neighbour: with flattering lips and with a double heart do they speak.

2 Peter 3:16 (KJV)
16 As also in all his epistles, speaking in them of these things; in which are some things hard to be understood, which they that are unlearned and unstable wrest, as they do also the other scriptures, unto their own destruction.

Remember Jesus has proven himself faithful so that engrafted and adopted sons would receive the anointing to be faithful through his obedience to the Father.

Week Twelve: Double Heart

Take comfort in the following passage:

Romans 8:1-6 (KJV)
1 There is therefore now no condemnation to them which are in Christ Jesus, who walk not after the flesh, but after the Spirit. 2 For the law of the Spirit of life in Christ Jesus hath made me free from the law of sin and death. 3 For what the law could not do, in that it was weak through the flesh, God sending his own Son in the likeness of sinful flesh, and for sin, condemned sin in the flesh: 4 That the righteousness of the law might be fulfilled in us, who walk not after the flesh, but after the Spirit. 5 For they that are after the flesh do mind the things of the flesh; but they that are after the Spirit the things of the Spirit. 6 For to be carnally minded is death; but to be spiritually minded is life and peace.

What Weights and Burdens Come to Mind to Lay Down?

_____

_____

YOUR PERSONAL COMMITMENT TO GOD

Thanksgiving – Praise – Worship Your Way into His Presence
Opening Prayer (Remember Put on Your Armour!)
Scripture(s) Reading

Call to Action for the Day
Will I chose to believe the truth I've discovered?
Will I allow the truth to change my thinking and my conduct?
We must adjust ourselves to the Bible— never the Bible to ourselves.
Closing Prayer

Week Twelve: Double Heart

GODS COMMITMENT TO YOU

Promises from the Father _____

_____

Priorities of the Day _____

_____

Benefits for the Day _____

_____

DECLARATIONS AND DECREES

Protection _____

_____

Strategies for the Day _____

_____

Week Twelve: Double Heart

PRAISE REPORT

Cool of the Day Revelation_____

WEEK Thirteen

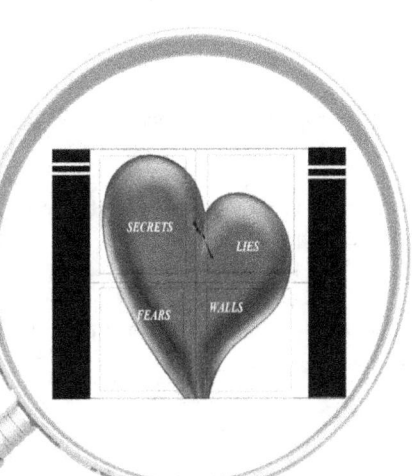

CALENDAR

Day		Sat	Sun	Mon	Tue	Wed	Thu	Fri
Date	Hour							
1st Watch	6–9 pm							
2nd Watch	9–12 am							
3rd Watch	12–3 am							
4th Watch	3–6 am							
5th Watch	6–9 am							
6th Watch	9–12 pm							
7th Watch	12–3 pm							
8th Watch	3–6 pm							

"...And what thou readest well, thou canst not too well understand;..."
Martin Luther

Weekly Plan Synopsis *(See Appendix for full plan)*

Day 1
Telling yourself and God the truth about where you are in your heart today! Repent and commit it to God.

Day 2
Pray Psalms 51 in the first person tense for yourself, no matter who has hurt or betrayed you.

Day 3
Continue as an action of intent to forgive. Forgiveness is not a feeling -- but a commandment (to do). Release yourself from the torment, you deserve it. Pray "By faith (trust in God's ability) I choose to forgive those who have caused me pain in Jesus Name. I forgive name them as an act of faith.

Day 4
Begin thanking God for restoring your peace and for his forgiveness because you held onto unforgiveness in your heart!

Day 5
Wherefore my dearly beloved, flee from idolatry. (I Corinthians 10:13-14) Anything that occupies the space in our heart that belongs to God is idolatry.

Day 6
Could you be the one to share the gospel with them and save them from a burning hell! Remember one plants, another waters, and God gives the increase!

Day 7
What fruit can you pick from the Tree of Life to feed your heart today get started feeding the scriptures to your heart to manifest that fruit.

Week Thirteen: Tender Heart

Reference: Weekly Plan Outline (See Appendix)

Every day tell yourself the truth, face that truth no matter how ugly it is, repent of it and commit it to God. This is an action not a feeling; you do it by faith continuously until you feel the release in your spirit or until it is no longer a chore but a pleasure!

What is a Tender Heart?
A Heart easily hurt, fragile and easily damaged.

Hebrew: racham rakh' ·am mercy, compassion, womb, bowels, pity, damsel, tender love

Greek: oiktirmon oik-te'r-mon merciful, of tender mercy

2 Kings 22:19 Because thine heart was tender, and thou hast humbled thyself before the LORD, when thou heardest what I spake against this place, and against the inhabitants thereof, that they should become a desolation and a curse, and hast rent thy clothes, and wept before me; I also have heard [thee], saith the LORD.

Remember Jesus has proven himself faithful so that engrafted and adopted sons would receive the anointing to be faithful through his obedience to the Father.

Week Thirteen: Tender Heart

Take comfort in the following passage:

2 Chronicles 34:27 Because thine heart was tender, and thou didst humble thyself before God, when thou heardest his words against this place, and against the inhabitants thereof, and humbledst thyself before me, and didst rend thy clothes, and weep before me; I have even heard [thee] also, saith the LORD.

What Weights and Burdens Come to Mind to Lay Down?

_____

_____

YOUR PERSONAL COMMITMENT TO GOD

Thanksgiving – Praise – Worship Your Way into His Presence
Opening Prayer (Remember Put on Your Armour!)
Scripture(s) Reading

Call to Action for the Day
Will I chose to believe the truth I've discovered?
Will I allow the truth to change my thinking and my conduct?
We must adjust ourselves to the Bible— never the Bible to ourselves.
Closing Prayer

Week Thirteen: Tender Heart

GODS COMMITMENT TO YOU

Promises from the Father _____

_____

Priorities of the Day_____

_____

Benefits for the Day_____

_____

DECLARATIONS AND DECREES

Protection_____

_____

Strategies for the Day_____

_____

Week Thirteen: Tender Heart

PRAISE REPORT

Cool of the Day Revelation_____

WEEK Fourteen

CALENDAR

Day		Sat	Sun	Mon	Tue	Wed	Thu	Fri
Date	Hour							
1st Watch	6–9 pm							
2nd Watch	9-12 am							
3rd Watch	12–3 am							
4th Watch	3–6 am							
5th Watch	6–9 am							
6th Watch	9–12 pm							
7th Watch	12 –3 pm							
8th Watch	3–6 pm							

"...And what thou understandest well, thou canst not too well teach;..."
Martin Luther

Weekly Plan Synopsis *(See Appendix for full plan)*

Day 1
Telling yourself and God the truth about where you are in your heart today! Repent and commit it to God.

Day 2
Pray Psalms 51 in the first person tense for yourself, no matter who has hurt or betrayed you.

Day 3
Continue as an action of intent to forgive. Forgiveness is not a feeling -- but a commandment (to do). Release yourself from the torment, you deserve it. Pray "By faith (trust in God's ability) I choose to forgive those who have caused me pain in Jesus Name. I forgive name them as an act of faith.

Day 4
Begin thanking God for restoring your peace and for his forgiveness because you held onto unforgiveness in your heart!

Day 5
Wherefore my dearly beloved, flee from idolatry. (I Corinthians 10:13-14) Anything that occupies the space in our heart that belongs to God is idolatry.

Day 6
Could you be the one to share the gospel with them and save them from a burning hell! Remember one plants, another waters, and God gives the increase!

Day 7
What fruit can you pick from the Tree of Life to feed your heart today get started feeding the scriptures to your heart to manifest that fruit.

Week Fourteen: Soft Heart

Reference: Weekly Plan Outline (See Appendix)

Every day tell yourself the truth, face that truth no matter how ugly it is, repent of it and commit it to God. This is an action not a feeling; you do it by faith continuously until you feel the release in your spirit or until it is no longer a chore but a pleasure!

What is a Soft Heart?

Hebrew: muwg müg melt, dissolve, faint, melt away, consumed, fainthearted, soft

Greek: muwg müg melt, dissolve, faint, melt away, consumed, fainthearted, soft

Job 23:16
For God maketh my heart soft, and the Almighty troubleth me:

Psalms 22:14
14 I am poured out like water, and all my bones are out of joint: my heart is like wax; it is melted in the midst of my bowels.

Ruth 1:20
20 And she said unto them, Call me not Naomi, call me Mara: for the Almighty hath dealt very bitterly with me.

Psalms 88:15
15 I am afflicted and ready to die from my youth up: while I suffer thy terrors I am distracted.
Remember Jesus has proven himself faithful so that engrafted and adopted sons would receive the anointing to be faithful through his obedience to the Father.

Week Fourteen: Soft Heart

Remember Jesus has proven himself faithful so that engrafted and adopted sons would receive the anointing to be faithful through his obedience to the Father.

Take comfort in the following passage:

Matthew 7:13-14
13 Enter ye in at the strait gate: for wide is the gate, and broad is the way, that leadeth to destruction, and many there be which go in thereat: 14 Because strait is the gate, and narrow is the way, which leadeth unto life, and few there be that find it.

What Weights and Burdens Come to Mind to Lay Down?

_____

_____

YOUR PERSONAL COMMITMENT TO GOD

Thanksgiving – Praise – Worship Your Way into His Presence
Opening Prayer (Remember Put on Your Armour!)
Scripture(s) Reading

Call to Action for the Day
Will I chose to believe the truth I've discovered?
Will I allow the truth to change my thinking and my conduct?
We must adjust ourselves to the Bible— never the Bible to ourselves.
Closing Prayer

Week Fourteen: Soft Heart

GODS COMMITMENT TO YOU

Promises from the Father _____

_____

Priorities of the Day_____

_____

Benefits for the Day_____

_____

DECLARATIONS AND DECREES

Protection_____

_____

Strategies for the Day_____

_____

Week Fourteen: Soft Heart

PRAISE REPORT

Cool of the Day Revelation _____

WEEK Fifteen

CALENDAR

Day		Sat	Sun	Mon	Tue	Wed	Thu	Fri
Date	**Hour**							
1st Watch	6–9 pm							
2nd Watch	9–12 am							
3rd Watch	12–3 am							
4th Watch	3–6 am							
5th Watch	6–9 am							
6th Watch	9–12 pm							
7th Watch	12–3 pm							
8th Watch	3–6 pm							

> *"...And what thou teachest well, thou canst not too well live."*
> *Martin Luther*

Weekly Plan Synopsis *(See Appendix for full plan)*

Day 1
Telling yourself and God the truth about where you are in your heart today! Repent and commit it to God.

Day 2
Pray Psalms 51 in the first person tense for yourself, no matter who has hurt or betrayed you.

Day 3
Continue as an action of intent to forgive. Forgiveness is not a feeling -- but a commandment (to do). Release yourself from the torment, you deserve it. Pray "By faith (trust in God's ability) I choose to forgive those who have caused me pain in Jesus Name. I forgive name them as an act of faith.

Day 4
Begin thanking God for restoring your peace and for his forgiveness because you held onto unforgiveness in your heart!

Day 5
Wherefore my dearly beloved, flee from idolatry. (I Corinthians 10:13-14) Anything that occupies the space in our heart that belongs to God is idolatry.

Day 6
Could you be the one to share the gospel with them and save them from a burning hell! Remember one plants, another waters, and God gives the increase!

Day 7
What fruit can you pick from the Tree of Life to feed your heart today get started feeding the scriptures to your heart to manifest that fruit.

Week Fifteen: Pure Heart

Reference: Weekly Plan Outline (See Appendix)

Every day tell yourself the truth, face that truth no matter how ugly it is, repent of it and commit it to God. This is an action not a feeling; you do it by faith continuously until you feel the release in your spirit or until it is no longer a chore but a pleasure!

What is a Pure Heart?
A Heart free from faults, sinless, chaste, containing nothing inappropriate or unnecessary.

Hebrew: bar
1) pure, clear, sincere, clean, empty

Greek: katharos
1) clean, pure, physically, purified by fire
2) ...like a vine cleansed by pruning...so fitted to bear fruit
1) clean ...imparts no uncleanness, ethically
1) free from corrupt desire, from sin and guilt
2) free from every admixture of what is false, sincere genuine
3) blameless, innocent, unstained with the guilt of anything

Psalms 24:4
He that hath clean hands, and a pure heart; who hath not lifted up his soul unto vanity, nor sworn deceitfully.

I Timothy 1:5
Now the end of the commandment is charity out of a pure heart, and [of] a good conscience, and [of] faith unfeigned:

Week Fifteen: Pure Heart

Remember Jesus has proven himself faithful so that engrafted and adopted sons would receive the anointing to be faithful through his obedience to the Father.

Take comfort in the following passages:
Matthew 5:8
Blessed are the pure in heart: for they shall see God.

I Peter 1:22-23
22 Seeing ye have purified your souls in obeying the truth through the Spirit unto unfeigned love of the brethren, see that ye love one another with a pure heart fervently: 23 Being born again, not of corruptible seed, but of incorruptible, by the word of God, which liveth and abideth for ever.

What Weights and Burdens Come to Mind to Lay Down?

_____

_____

YOUR PERSONAL COMMITMENT TO GOD

Thanksgiving – Praise – Worship Your Way into His Presence
Opening Prayer (Remember Put on Your Armour!)
Scripture(s) Reading

Call to Action for the Day
Will I chose to believe the truth I've discovered?
Will I allow the truth to change my thinking and my conduct?
We must adjust ourselves to the Bible— never the Bible to ourselves.
Closing Prayer

Week Fifteen: Pure Heart

GODS COMMITMENT TO YOU

Promises from the Father _____
_____

Priorities of the Day_____
_____

Benefits for the Day_____
_____

DECLARATIONS AND DECREES

Protection_____
_____

Strategies for the Day_____
_____

Week Fifteen: Pure Heart

PRAISE REPORT

Cool of the Day Revelation_____

WEEK Sixteen

CALENDAR

Day	♥	Sat	Sun	Mon	Tue	Wed	Thu	Fri
Date	**Hour**							
1st Watch	6–9 pm							
2nd Watch	9–12 am							
3rd Watch	12–3 am							
4th Watch	3–6 am							
5th Watch	6–9 am							
6th Watch	9–12 pm							
7th Watch	12–3 pm							
8th Watch	3–6 pm							

Never leave a passage of Scripture until it has said something to you.
Robert Cook

Weekly Plan Synopsis *(See Appendix for full plan)*

Day 1
Telling yourself and God the truth about where you are in your heart today! Repent and commit it to God.

Day 2
Pray Psalms 51 in the first person tense for yourself, no matter who has hurt or betrayed you.

Day 3
Continue as an action of intent to forgive. Forgiveness is not a feeling -- but a commandment (to do). Release yourself from the torment, you deserve it. Pray "By faith (trust in God's ability) I choose to forgive those who have caused me pain in Jesus Name. I forgive name them as an act of faith.

Day 4
Begin thanking God for restoring your peace and for his forgiveness because you held onto unforgiveness in your heart!

Day 5
Wherefore my dearly beloved, flee from idolatry. (I Corinthians 10:13-14) Anything that occupies the space in our heart that belongs to God is idolatry.

Day 6
Could you be the one to share the gospel with them and save them from a burning hell! Remember one plants, another waters, and God gives the increase!

Day 7
What fruit can you pick from the Tree of Life to feed your heart today get started feeding the scriptures to your heart to manifest that fruit.

Week Sixteen: Upright Heart

Reference: Weekly Plan Outline (See Appendix)

Every day tell yourself the truth, face that truth no matter how ugly it is, repent of it and commit it to God. This is an action not a feeling; you do it by faith continuously until you feel the release in your spirit or until it is no longer a chore but a pleasure!

What is an Upright Heart?
A Heart adhering to moral principles.

Hebrew: yashar
1) straight, upright, correct, right, uprightness, righteous, upright, that which is upright

Psalm 7:10
My defence [is] of God, which saveth the upright in heart.

Psalm 11:2
For, lo, the wicked bend [their] bow, they make ready their arrow upon the string, that they may privily shoot at the upright in heart.

Psalm 32:11
Be glad in the LORD, and rejoice, ye righteous: and shout for joy, all [ye that are] upright in heart.

I King 15:5
Because David did [that which was] right in the eyes of the LORD, and turned not aside from any [thing] that he commanded him all the days of his life, save only in the matter of Uriah the Hittite.

Week Sixteen: Upright Heart

Remember Jesus has proven himself faithful so that engrafted and adopted sons would receive the anointing to be faithful through his obedience to the Father.

Take comfort in the following passages:

Matthew 5:8
Blessed are the pure in heart: for they shall see God.

Deuteronomy 12:28
Observe and hear all these words which I command thee, that it may go well with thee, and with thy children after thee for ever, when thou doest [that which is] good and right in the sight of the LORD thy God.

What Weights and Burdens Come to Mind to Lay Down?

_____

_____

YOUR PERSONAL COMMITMENT TO GOD

Thanksgiving – Praise – Worship Your Way into His Presence
Opening Prayer (Remember Put on Your Armour!)
Scripture(s) Reading

Call to Action for the Day
Will I chose to believe the truth I've discovered?
Will I allow the truth to change my thinking and my conduct?
We must adjust ourselves to the Bible— never the Bible to ourselves.
Closing Prayer

Week Sixteen: Upright Heart

GODS COMMITMENT TO YOU

Promises from the Father _____

_____

Priorities of the Day_____

_____

Benefits for the Day_____

_____

DECLARATIONS AND DECREES

Protection_____

_____

Strategies for the Day_____

_____

Week Sixteen: Upright Heart

PRAISE REPORT

Cool of the Day Revelation_____

_____

_____

_____

_____

_____

_____

_____

_____

_____

_____

WEEK Seventeen

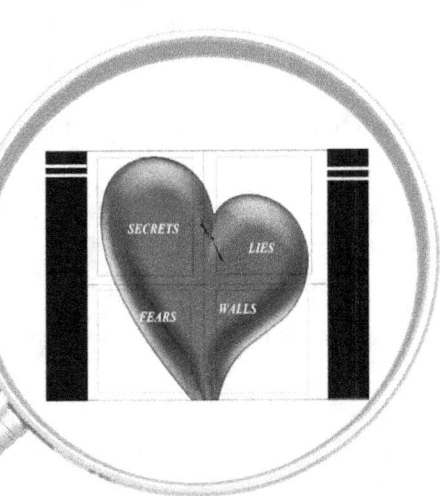

CALENDAR

Day		Sat	Sun	Mon	Tue	Wed	Thu	Fri
Date	Hour							
1st Watch	6–9 pm							
2nd Watch	9–12 am							
3rd Watch	12–3 am							
4th Watch	3–6 am							
5th Watch	6–9 am							
6th Watch	9–12 pm							
7th Watch	12–3 pm							
8th Watch	3–6 pm							

Study the Bible to be wise
Believe it to be safe
Practice it to be holy
Unknown

Weekly Plan Synopsis *(See Appendix for full plan)*

Day 1
Telling yourself and God the truth about where you are in your heart today! Repent and commit it to God.

Day 2
Pray Psalms 51 in the first person tense for yourself, no matter who has hurt or betrayed you.

Day 3
Continue as an action of intent to forgive. Forgiveness is not a feeling -- but a commandment (to do). Release yourself from the torment, you deserve it. Pray "By faith (trust in God's ability) I choose to forgive those who have caused me pain in Jesus Name. I forgive name them as an act of faith.

Day 4
Begin thanking God for restoring your peace and for his forgiveness because you held onto unforgiveness in your heart!

Day 5
Wherefore my dearly beloved, flee from idolatry. (I Corinthians 10:13-14) Anything that occupies the space in our heart that belongs to God is idolatry.

Day 6
Could you be the one to share the gospel with them and save them from a burning hell! Remember one plants, another waters, and God gives the increase!

Day 7
What fruit can you pick from the Tree of Life to feed your heart today get started feeding the scriptures to your heart to manifest that fruit.

Week Seventeen: Clean Heart

Reference: Weekly Plan Outline Day 1 through 7
(See Appendix)

Every day tell yourself the truth, face that truth no matter how ugly it is, repent of it and commit it to God. This is an action not a feeling; you do it by faith continuously until you feel the release in your spirit or until it is no longer a chore but a pleasure!

What is a Clean Heart?

a heart free from impurities or contamination.

Hebrew: barar bä ̇rar' pure, choice, chosen, clean, clearly, manifest, bright, purge out, polished, purge, purified

Greek: katharizo kä-thä-re'-zo cleanse, make clean, be clean, purge, purify

Psalm 51:10
Create in me a clean heart, O God; and renew a right spirit within me.

Psalm 73:1
A Psalm of Asaph. Truly God [is] good to Israel, [even] to such as are of a clean heart.

Week Seventeen: Clean Heart

Remember Jesus has proven himself faithful so that engrafted and adopted sons would receive the anointing to be faithful through his obedience to the Father.

Take comfort in the following passages:

Psalm 24:4
He that hath clean hands, and a pure heart; who hath not lifted up his soul unto vanity, nor sworn deceitfully.

Proverbs 20:9
Who can say, I have made my heart clean , I am pure from my sin?

What Weights and Burdens Come to Mind to Lay Down?

_____

_____

YOUR PERSONAL COMMITMENT TO GOD

Thanksgiving – Praise – Worship Your Way into His Presence
Opening Prayer (Remember Put on Your Armour!)
Scripture(s) Reading

Call to Action for the Day
Will I chose to believe the truth I've discovered?
Will I allow the truth to change my thinking and my conduct?
We must adjust ourselves to the Bible— never the Bible to ourselves.
Closing Prayer

Week Seventeen: Clean Heart

GODS COMMITMENT TO YOU

Promises from the Father _____

_____

Priorities of the Day_____

_____

Benefits for the Day_____

_____

DECLARATIONS AND DECREES

Protection_____

_____

Strategies for the Day_____

_____

Week Seventeen: Clean Heart
PRAISE REPORT

Cool of the Day Revelation _____

WEEK Eighteen

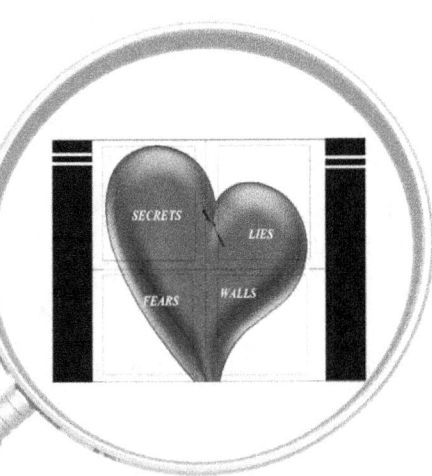

CALENDAR

Day		Sat	Sun	Mon	Tue	Wed	Thu	Fri
Date	Hour							
1st Watch	6–9 pm							
2nd Watch	9-12 am							
3rd Watch	12–3 am							
4th Watch	3–6 am							
5th Watch	6–9 am							
6th Watch	9–12 pm							
7th Watch	12–3 pm							
8th Watch	3–6 pm							

Sow a thought, reap an action.
Sow an action, reap a habit.
Sow a habit, reap a character.
Sow a character, reap a destiny!
Unknown

Weekly Plan Synopsis *(See Appendix for full plan)*

Day 1
Telling yourself and God the truth about where you are in your heart today! Repent and commit it to God.

Day 2
Pray Psalms 51 in the first person tense for yourself, no matter who has hurt or betrayed you.

Day 3
Continue as an action of intent to forgive. Forgiveness is not a feeling -- but a commandment (to do). Release yourself from the torment, you deserve it. Pray "By faith (trust in God's ability) I choose to forgive those who have caused me pain in Jesus Name. I forgive name them as an act of faith.

Day 4
Begin thanking God for restoring your peace and for his forgiveness because you held onto unforgiveness in your heart!

Day 5
Wherefore my dearly beloved, flee from idolatry. (I Corinthians 10:13-14) Anything that occupies the space in our heart that belongs to God is idolatry.

Day 6
Could you be the one to share the gospel with them and save them from a burning hell! Remember one plants, another waters, and God gives the increase!

Day 7
What fruit can you pick from the Tree of Life to feed your heart today get started feeding the scriptures to your heart to manifest that fruit.

Week Eighteen: Established Heart

Reference: Weekly Plan Outline (See Appendix)

Every day tell yourself the truth, face that truth no matter how ugly it is, repent of it and commit it to God. This is an action not a feeling; you do it by faith continuously until you feel the release in your spirit or until it is no longer a chore but a pleasure!

What is an Established Heart?

A Heart not changing or varying, stationary

Hebrew: Camak
1) to lean, lay, rest, support, put, uphold, lean upon
b) (Niphal) to support or brace oneself
c) (Piel) to sustain, refresh, revive

Greek: bebaioo
to make firm, establish, confirm, make sure

Hebrew 13:9 Be not carried about with divers and strange doctrines. For [it is] a good thing that the heart be established with grace; not with meats, which have not profited them that have been occupied therein.

Remember Jesus has proven himself faithful so that engrafted and adopted sons would receive the anointing to be faithful through his obedience to the Father.

Week Eighteen: Clean Heart

Take comfort in the following passage:

Psalm 112:8
His heart [is] established, he shall not be afraid, until he see [his desire] upon his enemies.

What Weights and Burdens Come to Mind to Lay Down?

_____

_____

YOUR PERSONAL COMMITMENT TO GOD

Thanksgiving – Praise – Worship Your Way into His Presence
Opening Prayer (Remember Put on Your Armour!)
Scripture(s) Reading

Call to Action for the Day
Will I chose to believe the truth I've discovered?
Will I allow the truth to change my thinking and my conduct?
We must adjust ourselves to the Bible— never the Bible to ourselves.
Closing Prayer

Week Eighteen: Clean Heart

GODS COMMITMENT TO YOU

Promises from the Father _____

_____

Priorities of the Day_____

_____

Benefits for the Day_____

_____

DECLARATIONS AND DECREES

Protection_____

_____

Strategies for the Day_____

_____

Week Eighteen: Clean Heart

PRAISE REPORT

Cool of the Day Revelation_____

WEEK Nineteen

CALENDAR

Day		Sat	Sun	Mon	Tue	Wed	Thu	Fri
Date	Hour							
1st Watch	6–9 pm							
2nd Watch	9–12 am							
3rd Watch	12–3 am							
4th Watch	3–6 am							
5th Watch	6–9 am							
6th Watch	9–12 pm							
7th Watch	12–3 pm							
8th Watch	3–6 pm							

When you arrive at a fork in the road, take it.
Yogi Berra

Weekly Plan Synopsis *(See Appendix for full plan)*

Day 1
Telling yourself and God the truth about where you are in your heart today! Repent and commit it to God.

Day 2
Pray Psalms 51 in the first person tense for yourself, no matter who has hurt or betrayed you.

Day 3
Continue as an action of intent to forgive. Forgiveness is not a feeling -- but a commandment (to do). Release yourself from the torment, you deserve it. Pray "By faith (trust in God's ability) I choose to forgive those who have caused me pain in Jesus Name. I forgive name them as an act of faith.

Day 4
Begin thanking God for restoring your peace and for his forgiveness because you held onto unforgiveness in your heart!

Day 5
Wherefore my dearly beloved, flee from idolatry. (I Corinthians 10:13-14) Anything that occupies the space in our heart that belongs to God is idolatry.

Day 6
Could you be the one to share the gospel with them and save them from a burning hell! Remember one plants, another waters, and God gives the increase!

Day 7
What fruit can you pick from the Tree of Life to feed your heart today get started feeding the scriptures to your heart to manifest that fruit.

Week Nineteen: Inditing Heart

Reference: Weekly Plan Outline (See Appendix)

Every day tell yourself the truth, face that truth no matter how ugly it is, repent of it and commit it to God. This is an action not a feeling; you do it by faith continuously until you feel the release in your spirit or until it is no longer a chore but a pleasure!

What is an Inditing Heart?
to keep moving and to be stirred

Hebrew: rachash rä ·khash'

Psalms 45:1-5 (KJV)
The majesty and grace of Christ's kingdom
To the chief Musician upon Shoshannim, for the sons of Korah, Maschil, A Song of loves.

    1 My heart is inditing a good matter: I speak of the things which I have made touching the king: my tongue is the pen of a ready writer. 2 Thou art fairer than the children of men: grace is poured into thy lips: therefore God hath blessed thee for ever. 3 Gird thy sword upon thy thigh, O most mighty, with thy glory and thy majesty. 4 And in thy majesty ride prosperously because of truth and meekness and righteousness; and thy right hand shall teach thee terrible things. 5 Thine arrows are sharp in the heart of the king's enemies; whereby the people fall under thee.

Remember Jesus has proven himself faithful so that engrafted and adopted sons would receive the anointing to be faithful through his obedience to the Father.

Week Nineteen: Inditing Heart

Take comfort in the following passage:

Matt 12:33-37 (KJV)
33 Either make the tree good, and his fruit good; or else make the tree corrupt, and his fruit corrupt: for the tree is known by his fruit. 34 O generation of vipers, how can ye, being evil, speak good things? for out of the abundance of the heart the mouth speaketh. 35 A good man out of the good treasure of the heart bringeth forth good things: and an evil man out of the evil treasure bringeth forth evil things. 36 But I say unto you, That every idle word that men shall speak, they shall give account thereof in the day of judgment. 37 For by thy words thou shalt be justified, and by thy words thou shalt be condemned.

What Weights and Burdens Come to Mind to Lay Down?

_____

_____

YOUR PERSONAL COMMITMENT TO GOD

Thanksgiving – Praise – Worship Your Way into His Presence
Opening Prayer (Remember Put on Your Armour!)
Scripture(s) Reading

Call to Action for the Day
Will I chose to believe the truth I've discovered?
Will I allow the truth to change my thinking and my conduct?
We must adjust ourselves to the Bible— never the Bible to ourselves.
Closing Prayer

Week Nineteen: Inditing Heart

GODS COMMITMENT TO YOU

Promises from the Father _____

_____

Priorities of the Day_____

_____

Benefits for the Day_____

_____

DECLARATIONS AND DECREES

Protection_____

_____

Strategies for the Day_____

_____

Week Nineteen: Inditing Heart

PRAISE REPORT

Cool of the Day Revelation_____

WEEK Twenty

CALENDAR

Day	♥	Sat	Sun	Mon	Tue	Wed	Thu	Fri
Date	Hour							
1st Watch	6–9 pm							
2nd Watch	9–12 am							
3rd Watch	12–3 am							
4th Watch	3–6 am							
5th Watch	6–9 am							
6th Watch	9–12 pm							
7th Watch	12–3 pm							
8th Watch	3–6 pm							

> *"I shall be telling this with a sigh*
> *Somewhere ages and ages hence:*
> *two roads diverged in a wood, and I --*
> *I took the one less traveled by,*
> *And that has made all the difference."*
> *Robert Frost*

Weekly Plan Synopsis *(See Appendix for full plan)*

Day 1
Telling yourself and God the truth about where you are in your heart today! Repent and commit it to God.

Day 2
Pray Psalms 51 in the first person tense for yourself, no matter who has hurt or betrayed you.

Day 3
Continue as an action of intent to forgive. Forgiveness is not a feeling -- but a commandment (to do). Release yourself from the torment, you deserve it. Pray "By faith (trust in God's ability) I choose to forgive those who have caused me pain in Jesus Name. I forgive name them as an act of faith.

Day 4
Begin thanking God for restoring your peace and for his forgiveness because you held onto unforgiveness in your heart!

Day 5
Wherefore my dearly beloved, flee from idolatry. (I Corinthians 10:13-14) Anything that occupies the space in our heart that belongs to God is idolatry.

Day 6
Could you be the one to share the gospel with them and save them from a burning hell! Remember one plants, another waters, and God gives the increase!

Day 7
What fruit can you pick from the Tree of Life to feed your heart today get started feeding the scriptures to your heart to manifest that fruit.

Week Twenty: Honest Heart

Reference: Weekly Plan Outline (See Appendix)

Every day tell yourself the truth, face that truth no matter how ugly it is, repent of it and commit it to God. This is an action not a feeling; you do it by faith continuously until you feel the release in your spirit or until it is no longer a chore but a pleasure!

What is a Honest **Heart?**
good, better, honest, meet, goodly,

Greek: kalos

Remember Jesus has proven himself faithful so that engrafted and adopted sons would receive the anointing to be faithful through his obedience to the Father.

At any time, the receptiveness of your heart will determine your response to God's word (Luke 8:5–18). If your heart is like the trampled ground, hardened by the sin of bitterness and unforgiveness, you will be unable to accept a message from God. Though you hear the words of the message, you will remain unchanged. If your heart is like the shallow soil on top of a rock, you will accept God's word in your mind, but the truth will not penetrate your heart to make a difference in your actions. A heart like thorny soil is a life that is distracted by the cares of the world; the pursuit of earthly pleasures prevents God's word from taking hold and producing righteousness. The heart that is like good soil receives a word from God, applies it, and brings forth fruit in due time. This is the heart that Jesus desires in us, for the fruit will be a Christlike life.

Any time you hear a word from God, whether through Bible reading, prayer, or worship, the way you respond will depend on how you have cultivated your heart (Hosea 10:12). How do you develop a heart that is like good soil? Repent of any bitterness, anger, or unforgiveness that is

Week Twenty: Honest Heart

hardening your heart. Meditate on God's word until it enters deep into your heart and not just your mind. When you read or hear a word from God, apply it to your life and let God bring His word into reality in your life (Gal. 6:9). Protect your lifestyle. See that you don't devote all of your energy to worldly concerns, rather than to pursuing your relationship with God. The condition of your heart will vary, depending on how you cultivate it. If it was receptive to a word from God yesterday, this does not guarantee it is receptive today. Daily prepare your heart for the word God has for you!
—Experiencing God Day by Day

Take comfort in the following passage(s):
 Colossians 1:6 Which is come unto you, as *it is* in all the world; and bringeth forth fruit, as *it doth* also in you, since the day ye heard *of it*, and knew the grace of God in truth:

What Weights and Burdens Come to Mind to Lay Down?

_____

_____

YOUR PERSONAL COMMITMENT TO GOD

Thanksgiving – Praise – Worship Your Way into His Presence
Opening Prayer (Remember Put on Your Armour!)
Scripture(s) Reading

Call to Action for the Day
Will I chose to believe the truth I've discovered?
Will I allow the truth to change my thinking and my conduct?
We must adjust ourselves to the Bible— never the Bible to ourselves.
Closing Prayer

Week Twenty: Honest Heart

GODS COMMITMENT TO YOU

Promises from the Father _____

_____

Priorities of the Day_____

_____

Benefits for the Day_____

_____

DECLARATIONS AND DECREES

Protection_____

_____

Strategies for the Day_____

_____

Week Twenty: Honest Heart
PRAISE REPORT

Cool of the Day Revelation_____

WEEK Twenty One

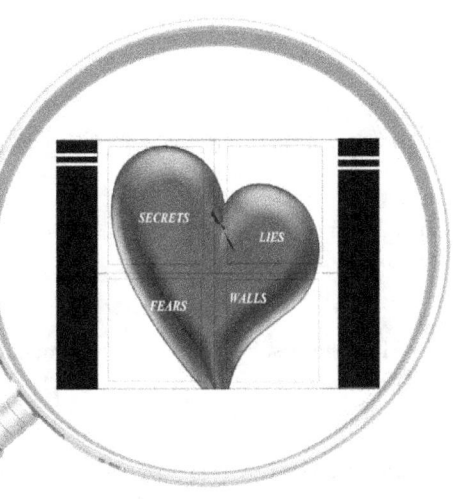

CALENDAR

Day		Sat	Sun	Mon	Tue	Wed	Thu	Fri
Date	Hour							
1st Watch	6–9 pm							
2nd Watch	9–12 am							
3rd Watch	12–3 am							
4th Watch	3–6 am							
5th Watch	6–9 am							
6th Watch	9–12 pm							
7th Watch	12–3 pm							
8th Watch	3–6 pm							

"While other books inform, and some few reform, this one book transforms."
A.T. Pierson

Weekly Plan Synopsis *(See Appendix for full plan)*

Day 1
Telling yourself and God the truth about where you are in your heart today! Repent and commit it to God.

Day 2
Pray Psalms 51 in the first person tense for yourself, no matter who has hurt or betrayed you.

Day 3
Continue as an action of intent to forgive. Forgiveness is not a feeling -- but a commandment (to do). Release yourself from the torment, you deserve it. Pray "By faith (trust in God's ability) I choose to forgive those who have caused me pain in Jesus Name. I forgive name them as an act of faith.

Day 4
Begin thanking God for restoring your peace and for his forgiveness because you held onto unforgiveness in your heart!

Day 5
Wherefore my dearly beloved, flee from idolatry. (I Corinthians 10:13-14) Anything that occupies the space in our heart that belongs to God is idolatry.

Day 6
Could you be the one to share the gospel with them and save them from a burning hell! Remember one plants, another waters, and God gives the increase!

Day 7
What fruit can you pick from the Tree of Life to feed your heart today get started feeding the scriptures to your heart to manifest that fruit.

Week Twenty-One: Wise Heart
Reference: Weekly Plan Outline (See Appendix)

Every day tell yourself the truth, face that truth no matter how ugly it is, repent of it and commit it to God. This is an action not a feeling; you do it by faith continuously until you feel the release in your spirit or until it is no longer a chore but a pleasure!

What is a Wise Heart?
wise, wise (man), a) skilful (in technical work), wise (in administration), shrewd, crafty, cunning, wily, subtle, learned, shrewd (class of men), prudent and wise (ethically and religiously)

Hebrew: chakam

Greek: syniemi sün-e'-a-me

Remember Jesus has proven himself faithful so that engrafted and adopted sons would receive the anointing to be faithful through his obedience to the Father.

Psalms 73:11

[11] And they say, How doth God know? and is there knowledge in the most High?

Ecclesiastes 9:1 [1] For all this I considered in my heart even to declare all this, that the righteous, and the wise, and their works, *are* in the hand of God: no man knoweth either love or hatred *by* all *that is* before them.

Week Twenty-One: Wise Heart

Take comfort in the following passage(s):

Eccl 10:1-2 (KJV)

² A wise man's heart *is* at his right hand; but a fool's heart at his left.

What Weights and Burdens Come to Mind to Lay Down?

_____

_____

YOUR PERSONAL COMMITMENT TO GOD

Thanksgiving – Praise – Worship Your Way into His Presence
Opening Prayer (Remember Put on Your Armour!)
Scripture(s) Reading

Call to Action for the Day
Will I chose to believe the truth I've discovered?
Will I allow the truth to change my thinking and my conduct?
We must adjust ourselves to the Bible— never the Bible to ourselves.
Closing Prayer

Week Twenty-One: Wise Heart

GODS COMMITMENT TO YOU

Promises from the Father _____

_____

Priorities of the Day_____

_____

Benefits for the Day_____

_____

DECLARATIONS AND DECREES

Protection_____

_____

Strategies for the Day_____

_____

Week Twenty-One: Wise Heart

PRAISE REPORT

Cool of the Day Revelation_____

WEEK Twenty Two

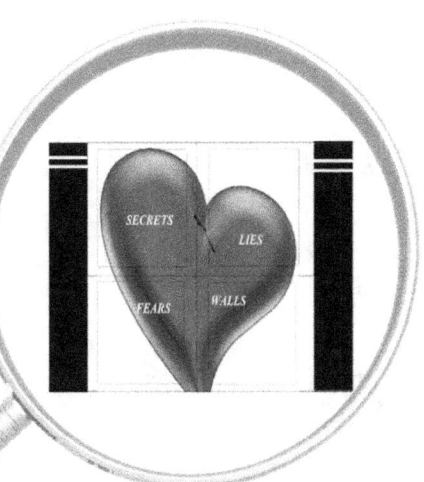

CALENDAR

Day		Sat	Sun	Mon	Tue	Wed	Thu	Fri
Date	**Hour**							
1st Watch	6–9 pm							
2nd Watch	9–12 am							
3rd Watch	12–3 am							
4th Watch	3–6 am							
5th Watch	6–9 am							
6th Watch	9–12 pm							
7th Watch	12–3 pm							
8th Watch	3–6 pm							

Read it to get the facts, study it to get the meaning, meditate on it to get the benefit.
David Shepherd

Weekly Plan Synopsis *(See Appendix for full plan)*

Day 1
Telling yourself and God the truth about where you are in your heart today! Repent and commit it to God.

Day 2
Pray Psalms 51 in the first person tense for yourself, no matter who has hurt or betrayed you.

Day 3
Continue as an action of intent to forgive. Forgiveness is not a feeling -- but a commandment (to do). Release yourself from the torment, you deserve it. Pray "By faith (trust in God's ability) I choose to forgive those who have caused me pain in Jesus Name. I forgive name them as an act of faith.

Day 4
Begin thanking God for restoring your peace and for his forgiveness because you held onto unforgiveness in your heart!

Day 5
Wherefore my dearly beloved, flee from idolatry. (I Corinthians 10:13-14) Anything that occupies the space in our heart that belongs to God is idolatry.

Day 6
Could you be the one to share the gospel with them and save them from a burning hell! Remember one plants, another waters, and God gives the increase!

Day 7
What fruit can you pick from the Tree of Life to feed your heart today get started feeding the scriptures to your heart to manifest that fruit.

Week Twenty-Two: Merry Heart
Reference: Weekly Plan Outline (See Appendix)

Every day tell yourself the truth, face that truth no matter how ugly it is, repent of it and commit it to God. This is an action not a feeling; you do it by faith continuously until you feel the release in your spirit or until it is no longer a chore but a pleasure!

What is a Merry Heart?
A Heart full of gaiety, glad and joyous.

Hebrew: sameach

Greek: euphraino
rejoice, be merry, make merry, fare, make glad

Remember Jesus has proven himself faithful so that engrafted and adopted sons would receive the anointing to be faithful through his obedience to the Father.

Proverbs 17:22
22 A merry heart doeth good *like* a medicine: but a broken spirit drieth the bones.

Proverbs 15:15
15 All the days of the afflicted *are* evil: but he that is of a merry heart *hath* a continual feast.

Week Twenty-Two: Merry Heart

Take comfort in the following passage(s):
Romans 5:1-5
1 Therefore being justified by faith, we have peace with God through our Lord Jesus Christ: **2** By whom also we have access by faith into this grace wherein we stand, and rejoice in hope of the glory of God. **3** And not only *so*, but we glory in tribulations also: knowing that tribulation worketh patience; **4** And patience, experience; and experience, hope: **5** And hope maketh not ashamed; because the love of God is shed abroad in our hearts by the Holy Ghost which is given unto us.

What Weights and Burdens Come to Mind to Lay Down?

_____

_____

YOUR PERSONAL COMMITMENT TO GOD

Thanksgiving – Praise – Worship Your Way into His Presence
Opening Prayer (Remember Put on Your Armour!)
Scripture(s) Reading

Call to Action for the Day
Will I chose to believe the truth I've discovered?
Will I allow the truth to change my thinking and my conduct?
We must adjust ourselves to the Bible— never the Bible to ourselves.
Closing Prayer

Week Twenty-Two: Merry Heart

GODS COMMITMENT TO YOU

Promises from the Father _____

_____

Priorities of the Day_____

_____

Benefits for the Day_____

_____

DECLARATIONS AND DECREES

Protection_____

_____

Strategies for the Day_____

_____

Week Twenty-Two: Merry Heart

PRAISE REPORT

Cool of the Day Revelation_____

WEEK Twenty Three

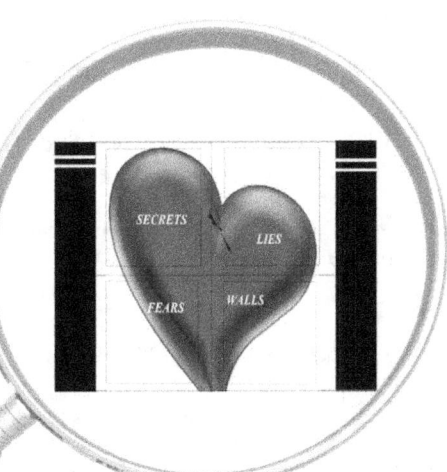

CALENDAR

Day	♥	Sat	Sun	Mon	Tue	Wed	Thu	Fri
Date	Hour							
1st Watch	6–9 pm							
2nd Watch	9–12 am							
3rd Watch	12–3 am							
4th Watch	3–6 am							
5th Watch	6–9 am							
6th Watch	9–12 pm							
7th Watch	12–3 pm							
8th Watch	3–6 pm							

Leave not off reading the Bible till you find your hearts warmed. Let it not only inform you but inflame you.
Thomas Watson

Weekly Plan Synopsis *(See Appendix for full plan)*

Day 1
Telling yourself and God the truth about where you are in your heart today! Repent and commit it to God.

Day 2
Pray Psalms 51 in the first person tense for yourself, no matter who has hurt or betrayed you.

Day 3
Continue as an action of intent to forgive. Forgiveness is not a feeling -- but a commandment (to do). Release yourself from the torment, you deserve it. Pray "By faith (trust in God's ability) I choose to forgive those who have caused me pain in Jesus Name. I forgive name them as an act of faith.

Day 4
Begin thanking God for restoring your peace and for his forgiveness because you held onto unforgiveness in your heart!

Day 5
Wherefore my dearly beloved, flee from idolatry. (I Corinthians 10:13-14) Anything that occupies the space in our heart that belongs to God is idolatry.

Day 6
Could you be the one to share the gospel with them and save them from a burning hell! Remember one plants, another waters, and God gives the increase!

Day 7
What fruit can you pick from the Tree of Life to feed your heart today get started feeding the scriptures to your heart to manifest that fruit.

Week Twenty-Three: Sorrowful Heart
Reference: Weekly Plan Outline (See Appendix)

Every day tell yourself the truth, face that truth no matter how ugly it is, repent of it and commit it to God. This is an action not a feeling; you do it by faith continuously until you feel the release in your spirit or until it is no longer a chore but a pleasure!

What is a Sorrowful Heart?
to be in pain, be sore, have pain, be sorrowful, to be in pain (physical), to be in pain (mental), to cause pain, hurt, mar, pain, mar (participle)

Hebrew: ka'ab sorrowful
to be in pain, be sore, have pain, be sorrowful

Greek: lypeo be sorrowful
grieve, make sorry, be sorry, sorrow, cause grief, be in heaviness

Remember Jesus has proven himself faithful so that engrafted and adopted sons would receive the anointing to be faithful through his obedience to the Father.

Proverbs 14:13-14 [13] Even in laughter the heart is sorrowful; and the end of that mirth *is* heaviness.

[14] The backslider in heart shall be filled with his own ways: and a good man *shall be satisfied* from himself.

Week Twenty-Three: Sorrowful Heart

Take comfort in the following passage(s):

Luke 16:25 ²⁵ But Abraham said, Son, remember that thou in thy lifetime receivedst thy good things, and likewise Lazarus evil things: but now he is comforted, and thou art tormented.

What Weights and Burdens Come to Mind to Lay Down?

_____

_____

"The Christian is personally related to the Lord of the universe, who is sovereign not only over all creation but also over every circumstance we experience…When God speaks a word to you, trust Him completely, for God never deceives His children. If God has indicated to you that He is going to do something, you can be absolutely confident that He will do it…God has given His word on many areas of life regarding things He *will* do. We can have confident hope in everything that He has promised." —Experiencing God Day by Day

YOUR PERSONAL COMMITMENT TO GOD

Thanksgiving – Praise – Worship Your Way into His Presence
Opening Prayer (Remember Put on Your Armour!)
Scripture(s) Reading

Call to Action for the Day
Will I chose to believe the truth I've discovered?
Will I allow the truth to change my thinking and my conduct?
We must adjust ourselves to the Bible— never the Bible to ourselves.
Closing Prayer

Week Twenty-Three: Sorrowful Heart

GODS COMMITMENT TO YOU

Promises from the Father _____

_____

Priorities of the Day_____

_____

Benefits for the Day_____

_____

DECLARATIONS AND DECREES

Protection_____

_____

Strategies for the Day_____

_____

Week Twenty-Three: Sorrowful Heart
PRAISE REPORT

Cool of the Day Revelation_____

WEEK Twenty Four

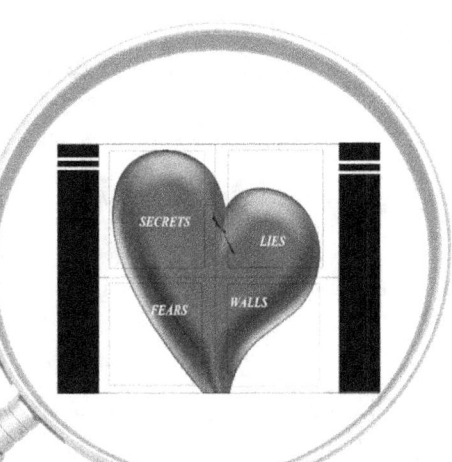

CALENDAR

Day		Sat	Sun	Mon	Tue	Wed	Thu	Fri
Date	Hour							
1st Watch	6–9 pm							
2nd Watch	9–12 am							
3rd Watch	12–3 am							
4th Watch	3–6 am							
5th Watch	6–9 am							
6th Watch	9–12 pm							
7th Watch	12–3 pm							
8th Watch	3–6 pm							

"To seek after mere notions of Truth, without an endeavor after an experience of its power in our hearts, is not the way to increase our understanding in spiritual things..."
John Owen

Weekly Plan Synopsis *(See Appendix for full plan)*

Day 1
Telling yourself and God the truth about where you are in your heart today! Repent and commit it to God.

Day 2
Pray Psalms 51 in the first person tense for yourself, no matter who has hurt or betrayed you.

Day 3
Continue as an action of intent to forgive. Forgiveness is not a feeling -- but a commandment (to do). Release yourself from the torment, you deserve it. Pray "By faith (trust in God's ability) I choose to forgive those who have caused me pain in Jesus Name. I forgive name them as an act of faith.

Day 4
Begin thanking God for restoring your peace and for his forgiveness because you held onto unforgiveness in your heart!

Day 5
Wherefore my dearly beloved, flee from idolatry. (I Corinthians 10:13-14) Anything that occupies the space in our heart that belongs to God is idolatry.

Day 6
Could you be the one to share the gospel with them and save them from a burning hell! Remember one plants, another waters, and God gives the increase!

Day 7
What fruit can you pick from the Tree of Life to feed your heart today get started feeding the scriptures to your heart to manifest that fruit.

Week Twenty-Four: Haughty Heart

Reference: Weekly Plan Outline (See Appendix)

Every day tell yourself the truth, face that truth no matter how ugly it is, repent of it and commit it to God. This is an action not a feeling; you do it by faith continuously until you feel the release in your spirit or until it is no longer a chore but a pleasure!

What is a Haughty Heart?
to be high, be exalted, to be haughty, be arrogant (bad sense), completion, destruction, consumption, annihilation, failing, pining

Hebrew: gabahh - haughty

Remember Jesus has proven himself faithful so that engrafted and adopted sons would receive the anointing to be faithful through his obedience to the Father.

Proverbs 18:12 [12] Before destruction the heart of man is haughty, and before honour *is* humility.

Psalms 131:1 [1] LORD, my heart is not haughty, nor mine eyes lofty: neither do I exercise myself in great matters, or in things too high for me.

I Samuel 16:14-15 [14] But the Spirit of the LORD departed from Saul, and an evil spirit from the LORD troubled him. [15] And Saul's servants said unto him, Behold now, an evil spirit from God troubleth thee.

Week Twenty-Four: Haughty Heart

Take comfort in the following passage(s):

I Samuel 16:13 Then Samuel took the horn of oil, and anointed him in the midst of his brethren: and the Spirit of the LORD came upon David from that day forward. So Samuel rose up, and went to Ramah.

Psalms 131:1-3 LORD, my heart is not haughty, nor mine eyes lofty: neither do I exercise myself in great matters, or in things too high for me. ² Surely I have behaved and quieted myself, as a child that is weaned of his mother: my soul *is* even as a weaned child. ³ Let Israel hope in the LORD from henceforth and for ever.

What Weights and Burdens Come to Mind to Lay Down?

_____

_____

YOUR PERSONAL COMMITMENT TO GOD

Thanksgiving – Praise – Worship Your Way into His Presence
Opening Prayer (Remember Put on Your Armour!)
Scripture(s) Reading

Call to Action for the Day
Will I chose to believe the truth I've discovered?
Will I allow the truth to change my thinking and my conduct?
We must adjust ourselves to the Bible— never the Bible to ourselves.
Closing Prayer

Week Twenty-Four: Haughty Heart

GODS COMMITMENT TO YOU

Promises from the Father _____

_____

Priorities of the Day_____

_____

Benefits for the Day_____

_____

DECLARATIONS AND DECREES

Protection_____

_____

Strategies for the Day_____

_____

Week Twenty-Four: Haughty Heart
PRAISE REPORT

Cool of the Day Revelation_____

WEEK Twenty Five

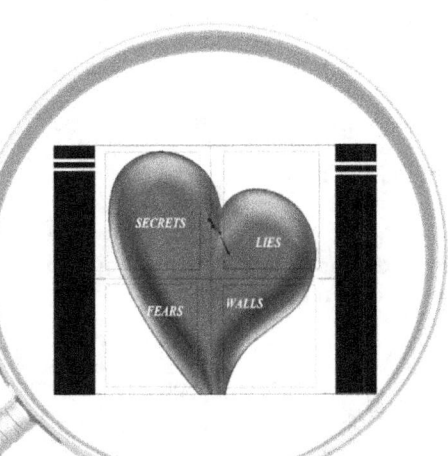

CALENDAR

Day		Sat	Sun	Mon	Tue	Wed	Thu	Fri
Date	Hour							
1st Watch	6–9 pm							
2nd Watch	9-12 am							
3rd Watch	12–3 am							
4th Watch	3–6 am							
5th Watch	6–9 am							
6th Watch	9–12 pm							
7th Watch	12–3 pm							
8th Watch	3–6 pm							

"...He alone is in a posture to learn from God, who sincerely gives up (surrenders, yields) his mind, conscience, and affections to the power and rule of what is revealed unto him..."
John Owen

Weekly Plan Synopsis *(See Appendix for full plan)*

Day 1
Telling yourself and God the truth about where you are in your heart today! Repent and commit it to God.

Day 2
Pray Psalms 51 in the first person tense for yourself, no matter who has hurt or betrayed you.

Day 3
Continue as an action of intent to forgive. Forgiveness is not a feeling -- but a commandment (to do). Release yourself from the torment, you deserve it. Pray "By faith (trust in God's ability) I choose to forgive those who have caused me pain in Jesus Name. I forgive name them as an act of faith.

Day 4
Begin thanking God for restoring your peace and for his forgiveness because you held onto unforgiveness in your heart!

Day 5
Wherefore my dearly beloved, flee from idolatry. (I Corinthians 10:13-14) Anything that occupies the space in our heart that belongs to God is idolatry.

Day 6
Could you be the one to share the gospel with them and save them from a burning hell! Remember one plants, another waters, and God gives the increase!

Day 7
What fruit can you pick from the Tree of Life to feed your heart today get started feeding the scriptures to your heart to manifest that fruit.

Week Twenty-Five: Failing Heart

Reference: Weekly Plan Outline (See Appendix)

Every day tell yourself the truth, face that truth no matter how ugly it is, repent of it and commit it to God. This is an action not a feeling; you do it by faith continuously until you feel the release in your spirit or until it is no longer a chore but a pleasure!

What is a Failing Heart?
failing, consumption, heart failing

Hebrew: killayown
Greek: apopsycho

Remember Jesus has proven himself faithful so that engrafted and adopted sons would receive the anointing to be faithful through his obedience to the Father.

Deuteronomy 28:65 And among these nations shalt thou find no ease, neither shall the sole of thy foot have rest: but the LORD shall give thee there a trembling heart, and failing of eyes, and sorrow of mind:

Luke 21:26 Men's hearts failing them for fear, and for looking after those things which are coming on the earth: for the powers of heaven shall be shaken.

Matthew 24:7-8 7 For nation shall rise against nation, and kingdom against kingdom: and there shall be famines, and pestilences, and earthquakes, in divers places. 8 All these are the beginning of sorrows.

Week Twenty-Five: Failing Heart

Take comfort in the following passage(s):

Mark 13:9-13 ⁹ But take heed to yourselves: for they shall deliver you up to councils; and in the synagogues ye shall be beaten: and ye shall be brought before rulers and kings for my sake, for a testimony against them. ¹⁰ And the gospel must first be published among all nations. ¹¹ But when they shall lead *you*, and deliver you up, take no thought beforehand what ye shall speak, neither do ye premeditate: but whatsoever shall be given you in that hour, that speak ye: for it is not ye that speak, but the Holy Ghost. ¹² Now the brother shall betray the brother to death, and the father the son; and children shall rise up against *their* parents, and shall cause them to be put to death. ¹³ And ye shall be hated of all *men* for my name's sake: but he that shall endure unto the end, the same shall be saved.

What Weights and Burdens Come to Mind to Lay Down?

_____

_____

YOUR PERSONAL COMMITMENT TO GOD

Thanksgiving – Praise – Worship Your Way into His Presence
Opening Prayer (Remember Put on Your Armour!)
Scripture(s) Reading

Call to Action for the Day
Will I chose to believe the truth I've discovered?
Will I allow the truth to change my thinking and my conduct?
We must adjust ourselves to the Bible— never the Bible to ourselves.
Closing Prayer

Week Twenty-Five: Failing Heart

GODS COMMITMENT TO YOU

Promises from the Father _____

_____

Priorities of the Day_____

_____

Benefits for the Day_____

_____

DECLARATIONS AND DECREES

Protection_____

_____

Strategies for the Day_____

_____

Week Twenty-Five: Failing Heart

PRAISE REPORT

Cool of the Day Revelation_____

WEEK Twenty Six

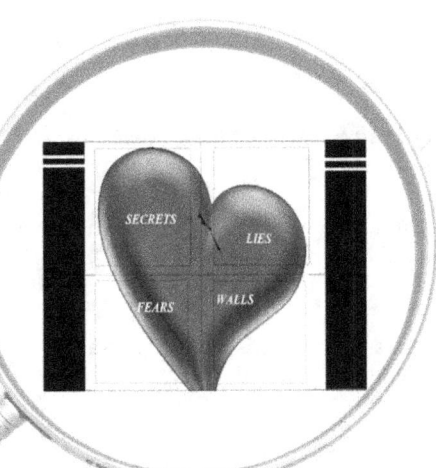

CALENDAR

Day		Sat	Sun	Mon	Tue	Wed	Thu	Fri
Date	**Hour**							
1st Watch	6–9 pm							
2nd Watch	9-12 am							
3rd Watch	12–3 am							
4th Watch	3–6 am							
5th Watch	6–9 am							
6th Watch	9–12 pm							
7th Watch	12–3 pm							
8th Watch	3–6 pm							

"...Men may have in their study of the Scriptures other ends also, as the profit and edification of others..."
John Owen

Weekly Plan Synopsis *(See Appendix for full plan)*

Day 1
Telling yourself and God the truth about where you are in your heart today! Repent and commit it to God.

Day 2
Pray Psalms 51 in the first person tense for yourself, no matter who has hurt or betrayed you.

Day 3
Continue as an action of intent to forgive. Forgiveness is not a feeling -- but a commandment (to do). Release yourself from the torment, you deserve it. Pray "By faith (trust in God's ability) I choose to forgive those who have caused me pain in Jesus Name. I forgive name them as an act of faith.

Day 4
Begin thanking God for restoring your peace and for his forgiveness because you held onto unforgiveness in your heart!

Day 5
Wherefore my dearly beloved, flee from idolatry. (I Corinthians 10:13-14) Anything that occupies the space in our heart that belongs to God is idolatry.

Day 6
Could you be the one to share the gospel with them and save them from a burning hell! Remember one plants, another waters, and God gives the increase!

Day 7
What fruit can you pick from the Tree of Life to feed your heart today get started feeding the scriptures to your heart to manifest that fruit.

Week Twenty-Six: Heavy Heart
Reference: Weekly Plan Outline (See Appendix)

Every day tell yourself the truth, face that truth no matter how ugly it is, repent of it and commit it to God. This is an action not a feeling; you do it by faith continuously until you feel the release in your spirit or until it is no longer a chore but a pleasure!

What is a Heavy Heart?
bad, disagreeable, malignant, unpleasant, evil (giving pain, unhappiness, misery), injury, wrong

Hebrew: kawbad

Remember Jesus has proven himself faithful so that engrafted and adopted sons would receive the anointing to be faithful through his obedience to the Father.

Isaiah 6:9-10 9 And he said, Go, and tell this people, Hear ye indeed, but understand not; and see ye indeed, but perceive not. 10 Make the heart of this people fat, and make their ears heavy, and shut their eyes; lest they see with their eyes, and hear with their ears, and understand with their heart, and convert, and be healed.

Isaiah 63:17 17 O LORD, why hast thou made us to err from thy ways, and hardened our heart from thy fear? Return for thy servants' sake, the tribes of thine inheritance.

Psalms 80:14-18 Return, we beseech thee, O God of hosts: look down from heaven, and behold, and visit this vine; 15 And the vineyard which thy right hand hath planted, and the branch *that* thou madest strong for thyself. 16 *It is* burned with fire, *it is* cut down: they perish at the rebuke of thy countenance. 17 Let thy hand be upon the man of thy right hand, upon the son of man *whom* thou madest strong for thyself. 18 So will not we go back from thee: quicken us, and we will call upon thy name.

Week Twenty-Six: Heavy Heart

Take comfort in the following passage(s):

Psalms 27:3-6 **3** Though an host should encamp against me, my heart shall not fear: though war should rise against me, in this *will* I *be* confident. **4** One *thing* have I desired of the LORD, that will I seek after; that I may dwell in the house of the LORD all the days of my life, to behold the beauty of the LORD, and to enquire in his temple. **5** For in the time of trouble he shall hide me in his pavilion: in the secret of his tabernacle shall he hide me; he shall set me up upon a rock. **6** And now shall mine head be lifted up above mine enemies round about me: therefore will I offer in his tabernacle sacrifices of joy; I will sing, yea, I will sing praises unto the LORD.

What Weights and Burdens Come to Mind to Lay Down?

_____

_____

YOUR PERSONAL COMMITMENT TO GOD

Thanksgiving – Praise – Worship Your Way into His Presence
Opening Prayer (Remember Put on Your Armour!)
Scripture(s) Reading

Call to Action for the Day
Will I chose to believe the truth I've discovered?
Will I allow the truth to change my thinking and my conduct?
We must adjust ourselves to the Bible— never the Bible to ourselves.
Closing Prayer

Week Twenty-Six: Heavy Heart

GODS COMMITMENT TO YOU

Promises from the Father _____

_____

Priorities of the Day_____

_____

Benefits for the Day_____

_____

DECLARATIONS AND DECREES

Protection_____

_____

Strategies for the Day_____

_____

Week Twenty-Six: Heavy Heart
PRAISE REPORT

Cool of the Day Revelation_____

WEEK Twenty Seven

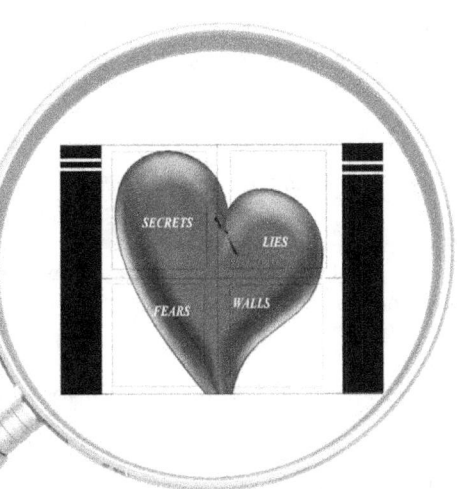

CALENDAR

Day		Sat	Sun	Mon	Tue	Wed	Thu	Fri
Date	Hour							
1st Watch	6–9 pm							
2nd Watch	9–12 am							
3rd Watch	12–3 am							
4th Watch	3–6 am							
5th Watch	6–9 am							
6th Watch	9–12 pm							
7th Watch	12–3 pm							
8th Watch	3–6 pm							

> *"...But if this conforming of their own souls unto the power of the Word be not fixed in the first place in their minds they do not strive lawfully, nor will they be crowned (!)..."*
> John Owen

Weekly Plan Synopsis *(See Appendix for full plan)*

Day 1
Telling yourself and God the truth about where you are in your heart today! Repent and commit it to God.

Day 2
Pray Psalms 51 in the first person tense for yourself, no matter who has hurt or betrayed you.

Day 3
Continue as an action of intent to forgive. Forgiveness is not a feeling -- but a commandment (to do). Release yourself from the torment, you deserve it. Pray "By faith (trust in God's ability) I choose to forgive those who have caused me pain in Jesus Name. I forgive name them as an act of faith.

Day 4
Begin thanking God for restoring your peace and for his forgiveness because you held onto unforgiveness in your heart!

Day 5
Wherefore my dearly beloved, flee from idolatry. (I Corinthians 10:13-14) Anything that occupies the space in our heart that belongs to God is idolatry.

Day 6
Could you be the one to share the gospel with them and save them from a burning hell! Remember one plants, another waters, and God gives the increase!

Day 7
What fruit can you pick from the Tree of Life to feed your heart today get started feeding the scriptures to your heart to manifest that fruit.

Week Twenty-Seven: Unsearchable Heart

Reference: Weekly Plan Outline (See Appendix)

Every day tell yourself the truth, face that truth no matter how ugly it is, repent of it and commit it to God. This is an action not a feeling; you do it by faith continuously until you feel the release in your spirit or until it is no longer a chore but a pleasure!

What is an Unsearchable Heart?
a search, investigation, searching, enquiry, thing to be searched out, without number

Hebrew: cheqer kha' ·ker
Greek: anexichniastos ä-ne-ksekh-ne'-ä-stos

Remember Jesus has proven himself faithful so that engrafted and adopted sons would receive the anointing to be faithful through his obedience to the Father.

Proverbs 25:1-5 **1** These *are* also proverbs of Solomon, which the men of Hezekiah king of Judah copied out.

2 *It is* the glory of God to conceal a thing: but the honour of kings *is* to search out a matter. **3** The heaven for height, and the earth for depth, and the heart of kings *is* unsearchable.

4 Take away the dross from the silver, and there shall come forth a vessel for the finer. **5** Take away the wicked *from* before the king, and his throne shall be established in righteousness.

Week Twenty-Seven: Unsearchable Heart

Take comfort in the following passage(s):

II Samuel 7:8-10 **8** Now therefore so shalt thou say unto my servant David, Thus saith the LORD of hosts, I took thee from the sheepcote, from following the sheep, to be ruler over my people, over Israel: **9** And I was with thee whithersoever thou wentest, and have cut off all thine enemies out of thy sight, and have made thee a great name, like unto the name of the great *men* that *are* in the earth. **10** Moreover I will appoint a place for my people Israel, and will plant them, that they may dwell in a place of their own, and move no more; neither shall the children of wickedness afflict them any more, as beforetime,

What Weights and Burdens Come to Mind to Lay Down?

_____

_____

YOUR PERSONAL COMMITMENT TO GOD

Thanksgiving – Praise – Worship Your Way into His Presence
Opening Prayer (Remember Put on Your Armour!)
Scripture(s) Reading

Call to Action for the Day
Will I chose to believe the truth I've discovered?
Will I allow the truth to change my thinking and my conduct?
We must adjust ourselves to the Bible— never the Bible to ourselves.
Closing Prayer

Week Twenty-Seven: Unsearchable Heart

GODS COMMITMENT TO YOU

Promises from the Father _____
_____

Priorities of the Day_____
_____

Benefits for the Day_____
_____

DECLARATIONS AND DECREES

Protection_____
_____

Strategies for the Day_____
_____

Week Twenty-Seven: Unsearchable Heart

PRAISE REPORT

Cool of the Day Revelation_____

WEEK Twenty Eight

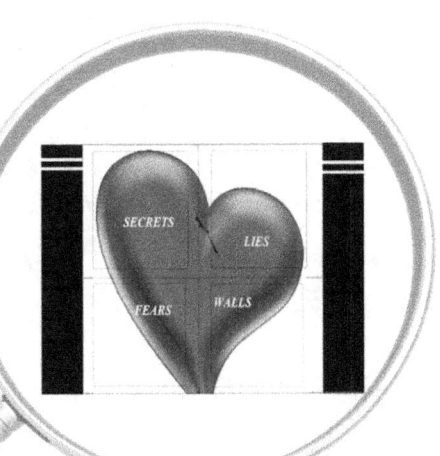

CALENDAR

Day	♥	Sat	Sun	Mon	Tue	Wed	Thu	Fri
Date	Hour							
1st Watch	6–9 pm							
2nd Watch	9-12 am							
3rd Watch	12–3 am							
4th Watch	3–6 am							
5th Watch	6–9 am							
6th Watch	9–12 pm							
7th Watch	12–3 pm							
8th Watch	3–6 pm							

"...And if at any time, when we study the Word, we have not this design expressly in our minds, yet if upon the discovery of any truth we endeavour not to have the likeness of it in our own hearts, we lose our principal advantage by it."
John Owen

Weekly Plan Synopsis *(See Appendix for full plan)*
Day 1
Telling yourself and God the truth about where you are in your heart today! Repent and commit it to God.

Day 2
Pray Psalms 51 in the first person tense for yourself, no matter who has hurt or betrayed you.

Day 3
Continue as an action of intent to forgive. Forgiveness is not a feeling -- but a commandment (to do). Release yourself from the torment, you deserve it. Pray "By faith (trust in God's ability) I choose to forgive those who have caused me pain in Jesus Name. I forgive name them as an act of faith.

Day 4
Begin thanking God for restoring your peace and for his forgiveness because you held onto unforgiveness in your heart!

Day 5
Wherefore my dearly beloved, flee from idolatry. (I Corinthians 10:13-14) Anything that occupies the space in our heart that belongs to God is idolatry.

Day 6
Could you be the one to share the gospel with them and save them from a burning hell! Remember one plants, another waters, and God gives the increase!

Day 7
What fruit can you pick from the Tree of Life to feed your heart today get started feeding the scriptures to your heart to manifest that fruit.

Week Twenty-Eight: Despiteful Heart

Reference: Weekly Plan Outline (See Appendix)

Every day tell yourself the truth, face that truth no matter how ugly it is, repent of it and commit it to God. This is an action not a feeling; you do it by faith continuously until you feel the release in your spirit or until it is no longer a chore but a pleasure!

What is a Despiteful Heart?
despiteful, injurious, contempt, destroy, by revenge, vengeance

Hebrew: she'at sheh ät'
Greek: hybristes hü-bre-sta's

Remember Jesus has proven himself faithful so that engrafted and adopted sons would receive the anointing to be faithful through his obedience to the Father.

Ezekiel 25:15 [15] Thus saith the Lord GOD; Because the Philistines have dealt by revenge, and have taken vengeance with a despiteful heart, to destroy *it* for the old hatred;

Ezekiel 36:5 Therefore thus saith the Lord GOD; Surely in the fire of my jealousy have I spoken against the residue of the heathen, and against all Idumea, which have appointed my land into their possession with the joy of all *their* heart, with despiteful minds, to cast it out for a prey.

Week Twenty-Eight: Despiteful Heart

Take comfort in the following passage(s):

Psalms 123:1-4 [1] Unto thee lift I up mine eyes, O thou that dwellest in the heavens. [2] Behold, as the eyes of servants *look* unto the hand of their masters, *and* as the eyes of a maiden unto the hand of her mistress; so our eyes *wait* upon the LORD our God, until that he have mercy upon us. [3] Have mercy upon us, O LORD, have mercy upon us: for we are exceedingly filled with contempt. [4] Our soul is exceedingly filled with the scorning of those that are at ease, *and* with the contempt of the proud.

What Weights and Burdens Come to Mind to Lay Down?

_____

_____

YOUR PERSONAL COMMITMENT TO GOD

Thanksgiving – Praise – Worship Your Way into His Presence
Opening Prayer (Remember Put on Your Armour!)
Scripture(s) Reading

Call to Action for the Day
Will I chose to believe the truth I've discovered?
Will I allow the truth to change my thinking and my conduct?
We must adjust ourselves to the Bible— never the Bible to ourselves.
Closing Prayer

Week Twenty-Eight: Despiteful Heart

GODS COMMITMENT TO YOU

Promises from the Father _____

_____

Priorities of the Day_____

_____

Benefits for the Day_____

_____

DECLARATIONS AND DECREES

Protection_____

_____

Strategies for the Day_____

_____

Week Twenty-Eight: Despiteful Heart

PRAISE REPORT

Cool of the Day Revelation_____

WEEK Twenty Nine

CALENDAR

Day	♥	Sat	Sun	Mon	Tue	Wed	Thu	Fri
Date	**Hour**							
1st Watch	6–9 pm							
2nd Watch	9–12 am							
3rd Watch	12–3 am							
4th Watch	3–6 am							
5th Watch	6–9 am							
6th Watch	9–12 pm							
7th Watch	12–3 pm							
8th Watch	3–6 pm							

Princes persecute me without cause, but (what's being contrasted?) my heart stands in awe of Thy words.
Psalms 119:161

Weekly Plan Synopsis *(See Appendix for full plan)*

Day 1
Telling yourself and God the truth about where you are in your heart today! Repent and commit it to God.

Day 2
Pray Psalms 51 in the first person tense for yourself, no matter who has hurt or betrayed you.

Day 3
Continue as an action of intent to forgive. Forgiveness is not a feeling -- but a commandment (to do). Release yourself from the torment, you deserve it. Pray "By faith (trust in God's ability) I choose to forgive those who have caused me pain in Jesus Name. I forgive name them as an act of faith.

Day 4
Begin thanking God for restoring your peace and for his forgiveness because you held onto unforgiveness in your heart!

Day 5
Wherefore my dearly beloved, flee from idolatry. (I Corinthians 10:13-14) Anything that occupies the space in our heart that belongs to God is idolatry.

Day 6
Could you be the one to share the gospel with them and save them from a burning hell! Remember one plants, another waters, and God gives the increase!

Day 7
What fruit can you pick from the Tree of Life to feed your heart today get started feeding the scriptures to your heart to manifest that fruit.

Week Twenty-Nine: Bitter Heart
Reference: Weekly Plan Outline (See Appendix)

Every day tell yourself the truth, face that truth no matter how ugly it is, repent of it and commit it to God. This is an action not a feeling; you do it by faith continuously until you feel the release in your spirit or until it is no longer a chore but a pleasure!

What is a Bitter Heart?
bitter, bitterness, bitterly, chafed, angry, discontented, heavy, bitter thing be bitter

Hebrew: mar

Greek: pikraino

Remember Jesus has proven himself faithful so that engrafted and adopted sons would receive the anointing to be faithful through his obedience to the Father.

Ecclesiastes 7:26 [26] And I find more bitter than death the woman, whose heart *is* snares and nets, *and* her hands *as* bands: whoso pleaseth God shall escape from her; but the sinner shall be taken by her.

Jeremiah 4:18 [18] Thy way and thy doings have procured these *things* unto thee; this *is* thy wickedness, because it is bitter, because it reacheth unto thine heart.

Jeremiah 2:19 [19] Thine own wickedness shall correct thee, and thy backslidings shall reprove thee: know therefore and see that *it is* an evil *thing* and bitter, that thou hast forsaken the LORD thy God, and that my fear *is* not in thee, saith the Lord GOD of hosts.

Week Twenty-Nine: Bitter Heart

Take comfort in the following passage(s):
Exodus 24:3 **3** And Moses came and told the people all the words of the LORD, and all the judgments: and all the people answered with one voice, and said, All the words which the LORD hath said will we do.

Hebrews 9:23-28   **23** *It was* therefore necessary that the patterns of things in the heavens should be purified with these; but the heavenly things themselves with better sacrifices than these. **24** For Christ is not entered into the holy places made with hands, *which are* the figures of the true; but into heaven itself, now to appear in the presence of God for us: **25** Nor yet that he should offer himself often, as the high priest entereth into the holy place every year with blood of others; **26** For then must he often have suffered since the foundation of the world: but now once in the end of the world hath he appeared to put away sin by the sacrifice of himself. **27** And as it is appointed unto men once to die, but after this the judgment: **28** So Christ was once offered to bear the sins of many; and unto them that look for him shall he appear the second time without sin unto salvation.

What Weights and Burdens Come to Mind to Lay Down?

_____

_____

YOUR PERSONAL COMMITMENT TO GOD
Thanksgiving – Praise – Worship Your Way into His Presence
Opening Prayer (Remember Put on Your Armour!)
Scripture(s) Reading

Call to Action for the Day
Will I chose to believe the truth I've discovered?
Will I allow the truth to change my thinking and my conduct?
We must adjust ourselves to the Bible— never the Bible to ourselves.
Closing Prayer

Week Twenty-Nine: Bitter Heart

GODS COMMITMENT TO YOU

Promises from the Father _____

_____

Priorities of the Day_____

_____

Benefits for the Day_____

_____

DECLARATIONS AND DECREES

Protection_____

_____

Strategies for the Day_____

_____

Week Twenty-Nine: Bitter Heart

PRAISE REPORT

Cool of the Day Revelation_____

WEEK Thirty

CALENDAR

Day		Sat	Sun	Mon	Tue	Wed	Thu	Fri
Date	**Hour**							
1st Watch	6–9 pm							
2nd Watch	9–12 am							
3rd Watch	12–3 am							
4th Watch	3–6 am							
5th Watch	6–9 am							
6th Watch	9–12 pm							
7th Watch	12–3 pm							
8th Watch	3–6 pm							

"...There is an awe of the Word, not that makes us shy of it, but tender of violating it, or doing anything contrary to it...."
Thomas Manton

Weekly Plan Synopsis *(See Appendix for full plan)*

Day 1
Telling yourself and God the truth about where you are in your heart today! Repent and commit it to God.

Day 2
Pray Psalms 51 in the first person tense for yourself, no matter who has hurt or betrayed you.

Day 3
Continue as an action of intent to forgive. Forgiveness is not a feeling -- but a commandment (to do). Release yourself from the torment, you deserve it. Pray "By faith (trust in God's ability) I choose to forgive those who have caused me pain in Jesus Name. I forgive name them as an act of faith.

Day 4
Begin thanking God for restoring your peace and for his forgiveness because you held onto unforgiveness in your heart!

Day 5
Wherefore my dearly beloved, flee from idolatry. (I Corinthians 10:13-14) Anything that occupies the space in our heart that belongs to God is idolatry.

Day 6
Could you be the one to share the gospel with them and save them from a burning hell! Remember one plants, another waters, and God gives the increase!

Day 7
What fruit can you pick from the Tree of Life to feed your heart today get started feeding the scriptures to your heart to manifest that fruit.

Week Thirty: New Heart

Reference: Weekly Plan Outline (See Appendix)

Every day tell yourself the truth, face that truth no matter how ugly it is, repent of it and commit it to God. This is an action not a feeling; you do it by faith continuously until you feel the release in your spirit or until it is no longer a chore but a pleasure!

What is a New Heart?
new, new thing, fresh

Hebrew: chadash

Remember Jesus has proven himself faithful so that engrafted and adopted sons would receive the anointing to be faithful through his obedience to the Father.

Ezekiel 18:31-32 [31] Cast away from you all your transgressions, whereby ye have transgressed; and make you a new heart and a new spirit: for why will ye die, O house of Israel? [32] For I have no pleasure in the death of him that dieth, saith the Lord GOD: wherefore turn *yourselves*, and live ye.

Ezekiel 36:26 [26] A new heart also will I give you, and a new spirit will I put within you: and I will take away the stony heart out of your flesh, and I will give you an heart of flesh.

Hosea 4:11 [11] Whoredom and wine and new wine take away the heart.

Week Thirty: New Heart

Take comfort in the following passage(s):
Ezekiel 11:19-20 [19] And I will give them one heart, and I will put a new spirit within you; and I will take the stony heart out of their flesh, and will give them an heart of flesh: [20] That they may walk in my statutes, and keep mine ordinances, and do them: and they shall be my people, and I will be their God.

What Weights and Burdens Come to Mind to Lay Down?

_____

_____

YOUR PERSONAL COMMITMENT TO GOD

Thanksgiving – Praise – Worship Your Way into His Presence
Opening Prayer (Remember Put on Your Armour!)
Scripture(s) Reading

Call to Action for the Day
Will I chose to believe the truth I've discovered?
Will I allow the truth to change my thinking and my conduct?
We must adjust ourselves to the Bible— never the Bible to ourselves.
Closing Prayer

Week Thirty: New Heart

GODS COMMITMENT TO YOU

Promises from the Father _____

_____

Priorities of the Day_____

_____

Benefits for the Day_____

_____

DECLARATIONS AND DECREES

Protection_____

_____

Strategies for the Day_____

_____

Week Thirty: New Heart

PRAISE REPORT

Cool of the Day Revelation_____

WEEK Thirty One

CALENDAR

Day	♥	Sat	Sun	Mon	Tue	Wed	Thu	Fri
Date	Hour							
1st Watch	6–9 pm							
2nd Watch	9-12 am							
3rd Watch	12–3 am							
4th Watch	3–6 am							
5th Watch	6–9 am							
6th Watch	9–12 pm							
7th Watch	12–3 pm							
8th Watch	3–6 pm							

"...This is not the fruit of slavish fear, but of holy love; it is not afraid of the Word, but delighting in it, as it discovers the mind of God to us; as in the next verse it is written, "I rejoice at Thy word."..."
Thomas Manton

Weekly Plan Synopsis *(See Appendix for full plan)*

Day 1
Telling yourself and God the truth about where you are in your heart today! Repent and commit it to God.

Day 2
Pray Psalms 51 in the first person tense for yourself, no matter who has hurt or betrayed you.

Day 3
Continue as an action of intent to forgive. Forgiveness is not a feeling -- but a commandment (to do). Release yourself from the torment, you deserve it. Pray "By faith (trust in God's ability) I choose to forgive those who have caused me pain in Jesus Name. I forgive name them as an act of faith.

Day 4
Begin thanking God for restoring your peace and for his forgiveness because you held onto unforgiveness in your heart!

Day 5
Wherefore my dearly beloved, flee from idolatry. (I Corinthians 10:13-14) Anything that occupies the space in our heart that belongs to God is idolatry.

Day 6
Could you be the one to share the gospel with them and save them from a burning hell! Remember one plants, another waters, and God gives the increase!

Day 7
What fruit can you pick from the Tree of Life to feed your heart today get started feeding the scriptures to your heart to manifest that fruit.

Week Thirty-One: Strong Heart

Reference: Weekly Plan Outline (See Appendix)

Every day tell yourself the truth, face that truth no matter how ugly it is, repent of it and commit it to God. This is an action not a feeling; you do it by faith continuously until you feel the release in your spirit or until it is no longer a chore but a pleasure!

What is a Strong Heart?
strength, strong, being strong, force, mighty, mighty man, strong, valiant, ... ones, mighties, man, valiant men, strong man, upright man , champion, chief, excel, giant, possible, able, mighty, strong, could, power, mighty man

Hebrew: chezqah & gibbowr ghib ·bore'
Greek: dynatos

Remember Jesus has proven himself faithful so that engrafted and adopted sons would receive the anointing to be faithful through his obedience to the Father.

II Chronicles 16:9 **9** For the eyes of the LORD run to and fro throughout the whole earth, to shew himself strong in the behalf of *them* whose heart *is* perfect toward him. Herein thou hast done foolishly: therefore from henceforth thou shalt have wars.

II Chronicles 26:16-17 **16** But when he was strong, his heart was lifted up to *his* destruction: for he transgressed against the LORD his God, and went into the temple of the LORD to burn incense upon the altar of incense. [1]

Week Thirty-One: Strong Heart

Take comfort in the following passage(s):
Galatian 3:6-11 **6** Even as Abraham believed God, and it was accounted to him for righteousness. **7** Know ye therefore that they which are of faith, the same are the children of Abraham. **8** And the scripture, foreseeing that God would justify the heathen through faith, preached before the gospel unto Abraham, *saying*, In thee shall all nations be blessed. **9** So then they which be of faith are blessed with faithful Abraham. **10** For as many as are of the works of the law are under the curse: for it is written, Cursed *is* every one that continueth not in all things which are written in the book of the law to do them. **11** But that no man is justified by the law in the sight of God, *it is* evident: for, The just shall live by faith.

What Weights and Burdens Come to Mind to Lay Down?

_____

_____

YOUR PERSONAL COMMITMENT TO GOD

Thanksgiving – Praise – Worship Your Way into His Presence
Opening Prayer (Remember Put on Your Armour!)
Scripture(s) Reading

Call to Action for the Day
Will I chose to believe the truth I've discovered?
Will I allow the truth to change my thinking and my conduct?
We must adjust ourselves to the Bible— never the Bible to ourselves.
Closing Prayer

Week Thirty-One: Strong Heart

GODS COMMITMENT TO YOU

Promises from the Father _____

_____

Priorities of the Day_____

_____

Benefits for the Day_____

_____

DECLARATIONS AND DECREES

Protection_____

_____

Strategies for the Day_____

_____

Week Thirty-One: Strong Heart

PRAISE REPORT

Cool of the Day Revelation_____

WEEK Thirty Two

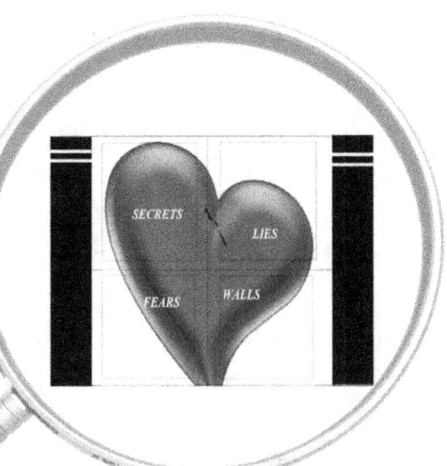

CALENDAR

Day		Sat	Sun	Mon	Tue	Wed	Thu	Fri
Date	Hour							
1st Watch	6–9 pm							
2nd Watch	9–12 am							
3rd Watch	12–3 am							
4th Watch	3–6 am							
5th Watch	6–9 am							
6th Watch	9–12 pm							
7th Watch	12–3 pm							
8th Watch	3–6 pm							

"...This awe is called by a proper name, reverence, or godly fear; when we consider Whose Word it is, namely, the Word of the Lord, Who is our God, and has a right to command what He pleases;..."
                                        Thomas Manton

Weekly Plan Synopsis *(See Appendix for full plan)*

Day 1
Telling yourself and God the truth about where you are in your heart today! Repent and commit it to God.

Day 2
Pray Psalms 51 in the first person tense for yourself, no matter who has hurt or betrayed you.

Day 3
Continue as an action of intent to forgive. Forgiveness is not a feeling -- but a commandment (to do). Release yourself from the torment, you deserve it. Pray "By faith (trust in God's ability) I choose to forgive those who have caused me pain in Jesus Name. I forgive name them as an act of faith.

Day 4
Begin thanking God for restoring your peace and for his forgiveness because you held onto unforgiveness in your heart!

Day 5
Wherefore my dearly beloved, flee from idolatry. (I Corinthians 10:13-14) Anything that occupies the space in our heart that belongs to God is idolatry.

Day 6
Could you be the one to share the gospel with them and save them from a burning hell! Remember one plants, another waters, and God gives the increase!

Day 7
What fruit can you pick from the Tree of Life to feed your heart today get started feeding the scriptures to your heart to manifest that fruit.

Week Thirty-Two: One Heart
Reference: Weekly Plan Outline (See Appendix)

Every day tell yourself the truth, face that truth no matter how ugly it is, repent of it and commit it to God. This is an action not a feeling; you do it by faith continuously until you feel the release in your spirit or until it is no longer a chore but a pleasure!

What is a One Heart?
denotes the centre of all physical and spiritual life, the vigour and sense of physical life, the centre and seat of spiritual life, the soul or mind, as it is the fountain and seat of the thoughts, passions, desires, appetites, affections, purposes, endeavours, of the understanding, the faculty and seat of the intelligence, of the will and character, of the soul so far as it is affected and stirred in a bad way or good, or of the soul as the seat of the sensibilities, affections, emotions, desires, appetites, passions, of the middle or central or inmost part of anything, even though inanimate, (Greek) transform, transfer in a figure, transform (one's) self, change

Hebrew: kardia

Greek: metaschematizo me-tä-skha-mä-te'-zo

Remember Jesus has proven himself faithful so that engrafted and adopted sons would receive the anointing to be faithful through his obedience to the Father.

Ezekiel 11:19-20 [19] And I will give them one heart, and I will put a new spirit within you; and I will take the stony heart out of their flesh, and will give them an heart of flesh: [20] That they may walk in my statutes, and keep mine ordinances, and do them: and they shall be my people, and I will be their God

Week Thirty-Two: One Heart

Take comfort in the following passage(s):
Jeremiah 32:38-42 And they shall be my people, and I will be their God: ³⁹ And I will give them one heart, and one way, that they may fear me for ever, for the good of them, and of their children after them: ⁴⁰ And I will make an everlasting covenant with them, that I will not turn away from them, to do them good; but I will put my fear in their hearts, that they shall not depart from me. ⁴¹ Yea, I will rejoice over them to do them good, and I will plant them in this land assuredly with my whole heart and with my whole soul. ⁴² For thus saith the LORD; Like as I have brought all this great evil upon this people, so will I bring upon them all the good that I have promised them.

What Weights and Burdens Come to Mind to Lay Down?

_____

_____

YOUR PERSONAL COMMITMENT TO GOD

Thanksgiving – Praise – Worship Your Way into His Presence
Opening Prayer (Remember Put on Your Armour!)
Scripture(s) Reading

Call to Action for the Day
Will I chose to believe the truth I've discovered?
Will I allow the truth to change my thinking and my conduct?
We must adjust ourselves to the Bible— never the Bible to ourselves.
Closing Prayer

Week Thirty-Two: One Heart

GODS COMMITMENT TO YOU

Promises from the Father _____

_____

Priorities of the Day _____

_____

Benefits for the Day _____

_____

DECLARATIONS AND DECREES

Protection _____

_____

Strategies for the Day _____

_____

Week Thirty-Two: One Heart

PRAISE REPORT

Cool of the Day Revelation_____

WEEK Thirty Three

CALENDAR

Day	♥	Sat	Sun	Mon	Tue	Wed	Thu	Fri
Date	**Hour**							
1st Watch	6–9 pm							
2nd Watch	9–12 am							
3rd Watch	12–3 am							
4th Watch	3–6 am							
5th Watch	6–9 am							
6th Watch	9–12 pm							
7th Watch	12–3 pm							
8th Watch	3–6 pm							

"...to Whose will and word we have already yielded obedience, and devoted ourselves to walk worthy of Him in all well pleasing..."
Thomas Manton

Weekly Plan Synopsis *(See Appendix for full plan)*

Day 1
Telling yourself and God the truth about where you are in your heart today! Repent and commit it to God.

Day 2
Pray Psalms 51 in the first person tense for yourself, no matter who has hurt or betrayed you.

Day 3
Continue as an action of intent to forgive. Forgiveness is not a feeling -- but a commandment (to do). Release yourself from the torment, you deserve it. Pray "By faith (trust in God's ability) I choose to forgive those who have caused me pain in Jesus Name. I forgive name them as an act of faith.

Day 4
Begin thanking God for restoring your peace and for his forgiveness because you held onto unforgiveness in your heart!

Day 5
Wherefore my dearly beloved, flee from idolatry. (I Corinthians 10:13-14) Anything that occupies the space in our heart that belongs to God is idolatry.

Day 6
Could you be the one to share the gospel with them and save them from a burning hell! Remember one plants, another waters, and God gives the increase!

Day 7
What fruit can you pick from the Tree of Life to feed your heart today get started feeding the scriptures to your heart to manifest that fruit.

Week Thirty-Three: Uncircumcised Heart
Reference: Weekly Plan Outline (See Appendix)

Every day tell yourself the truth, face that truth no matter how ugly it is, repent of it and commit it to God. This is an action not a feeling; you do it by faith continuously until you feel the release in your spirit or until it is no longer a chore but a pleasure!

What is an Uncircumcised Heart?
Metamorphically: those whose heart and ears are covered, whose soul and senses are closed to divine admonition

Hebrew: `arel ä ·ral'
Greek: aperitmetos

Remember Jesus has proven himself faithful so that engrafted and adopted sons would receive the anointing to be faithful through his obedience to the Father.

Jeremiah 9:26 Egypt, and Judah, and Edom, and the children of Ammon, and Moab, and all *that are* in the utmost corners, that dwell in the wilderness: for all *these* nations *are* uncircumcised, and all the house of Israel *are* uncircumcised in the heart.

Ezekiel 44:7-9 ⁷ In that ye have brought *into my sanctuary* strangers, uncircumcised in heart, and uncircumcised in flesh, to be in my sanctuary, to pollute it, *even* my house, when ye offer my bread, the fat and the blood, and they have broken my covenant because of all your abominations. ⁸ And ye have not kept the charge of mine holy things: but ye have set keepers of my charge in my sanctuary for yourselves. ⁹ Thus saith the Lord GOD; No stranger, uncircumcised in heart, nor uncircumcised in flesh, shall enter into my sanctuary, of any stranger that *is* among the children of Israel.

Week Thirty-Three: Uncircumcised Heart

[39] To whom our fathers would not obey, but thrust *him* from them, and in their hearts turned back again into Egypt,

Acts 7:39 (KJV)

Take comfort in the following passage(s):
I Samuel 16:7 "...for *the LORD seeth* not as man seeth; for man looketh on the outward appearance, but the LORD looketh on the heart."

"Only God knows the potential of each believer. We can project what we think God might do in someone's life, but we have no way of knowing. We see only outward appearances and behavior, whereas God looks at the heart There may be some around you in whom you have little confidence, though they claim to be Christians. Be assured that if God could turn the proud and murderous Saul into one of the greatest saints in history, He is equally capable of redeeming those around you.."—Experiencing God Day by Day

What Weights and Burdens Come to Mind to Lay Down?

_____

_____

YOUR PERSONAL COMMITMENT TO GOD
Thanksgiving – Praise – Worship Your Way into His Presence
Opening Prayer (Remember Put on Your Armour!)
Scripture(s) Reading

Call to Action for the Day
Will I chose to believe the truth I've discovered?
Will I allow the truth to change my thinking and my conduct?
We must adjust ourselves to the Bible— never the Bible to ourselves.
Closing Prayer

Week Thirty-Three: Uncircumcised Heart

GODS COMMITMENT TO YOU

Promises from the Father _____

_____

Priorities of the Day_____

_____

Benefits for the Day_____

_____

DECLARATIONS AND DECREES

Protection_____

_____

Strategies for the Day_____

_____

Week Thirty-Three: Uncircumcised Heart

PRAISE REPORT

Cool of the Day Revelation _____

WEEK Thirty Four

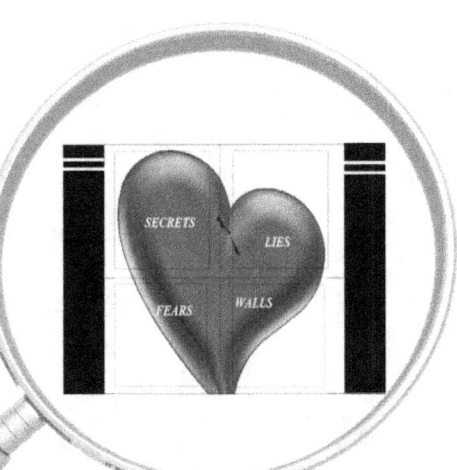

CALENDAR

Day	♥	Sat	Sun	Mon	Tue	Wed	Thu	Fri
Date	Hour							
1st Watch	6–9 pm							
2nd Watch	9–12 am							
3rd Watch	12–3 am							
4th Watch	3–6 am							
5th Watch	6–9 am							
6th Watch	9–12 pm							
7th Watch	12–3 pm							
8th Watch	3–6 pm							

> *"...who can find us out in all our failings, as knowing our very thoughts afar of (Psalms 139:2),..."*
> Thomas Manton

Weekly Plan Synopsis *(See Appendix for full plan)*

Day 1
Telling yourself and God the truth about where you are in your heart today! Repent and commit it to God.

Day 2
Pray Psalms 51 in the first person tense for yourself, no matter who has hurt or betrayed you.

Day 3
Continue as an action of intent to forgive. Forgiveness is not a feeling -- but a commandment (to do). Release yourself from the torment, you deserve it. Pray "By faith (trust in God's ability) I choose to forgive those who have caused me pain in Jesus Name. I forgive name them as an act of faith.

Day 4
Begin thanking God for restoring your peace and for his forgiveness because you held onto unforgiveness in your heart!

Day 5
Wherefore my dearly beloved, flee from idolatry. (I Corinthians 10:13-14) Anything that occupies the space in our heart that belongs to God is idolatry.

Day 6
Could you be the one to share the gospel with them and save them from a burning hell! Remember one plants, another waters, and God gives the increase!

Day 7
What fruit can you pick from the Tree of Life to feed your heart today get started feeding the scriptures to your heart to manifest that fruit.

Week Thirty-Four: Lowly Heart
Reference: Weekly Plan Outline (See Appendix)

Every day tell yourself the truth, face that truth no matter how ugly it is, repent of it and commit it to God. This is an action not a feeling; you do it by faith continuously until you feel the release in your spirit or until it is no longer a chore but a pleasure!

What is a Lowly Heart?
humble, poor, lowly, gentle, mild, meek

Hebrew: `anav ä ·näv'

Greek: praos prä'-os

Remember Jesus has proven himself faithful so that engrafted and adopted sons would receive the anointing to be faithful through his obedience to the Father.

Matthew 11:29 Take my yoke upon you, and learn of me; for I am meek and lowly in heart: and ye shall find rest unto your souls.

Remember Jesus has proven himself faithful so that engrafted and adopted sons would receive the anointing to be faithful through his obedience to the Father.

Psalms 22:26-28
26 The meek shall eat and be satisfied: they shall praise the LORD that seek him: your heart shall live for ever. 27 All the ends of the world shall remember and turn unto the LORD: and all the kindreds of the nations shall worship before thee. 28 For the kingdom is the LORD'S: and he is the governor among the nations.

Week Thirty-Four: Lowly Heart

Take comfort in the following passage(s):

1 Peter 3:4 [4] But *let it be* the hidden man of the heart, in that which is not corruptible, *even the ornament* of a meek and quiet spirit, which is in the sight of God of great price.

Matthew 11:29-30 [29] Take my yoke upon you, and learn of me; for I am meek and lowly in heart: and ye shall find rest unto your souls. [30] For my yoke *is* easy, and my burden is light.

What Weights and Burdens Come to Mind to Lay Down?

_____

_____

YOUR PERSONAL COMMITMENT TO GOD
Thanksgiving – Praise – Worship Your Way into His Presence
Opening Prayer (Remember Put on Your Armour!)
Scripture(s) Reading

Call to Action for the Day
Will I chose to believe the truth I've discovered?
Will I allow the truth to change my thinking and my conduct?
We must adjust ourselves to the Bible— never the Bible to ourselves.
Closing Prayer

Week Thirty-Four: Lowly Heart

GODS COMMITMENT TO YOU

Promises from the Father _____

_____

Priorities of the Day_____

_____

Benefits for the Day_____

_____

DECLARATIONS AND DECREES

Protection_____

_____

Strategies for the Day_____

_____

Week Thirty-Four: Lowly Heart
PRAISE REPORT

Cool of the Day Revelation_____

_____

_____

_____

_____

_____

_____

_____

_____

_____

_____

WEEK Thirty Five

CALENDAR

Day		Sat	Sun	Mon	Tue	Wed	Thu	Fri
Date	Hour							
1st Watch	6–9 pm							
2nd Watch	9–12 am							
3rd Watch	12–3 am							
4th Watch	3–6 am							
5th Watch	6–9 am							
6th Watch	9–12 pm							
7th Watch	12–3 pm							
8th Watch	3–6 pm							

"...and having all our ways before Him, and being one of Whom we read, --
"He is a holy God; He is a jealous God;..."
Thomas Manton

Weekly Plan Synopsis *(See Appendix for full plan)*

Day 1
Telling yourself and God the truth about where you are in your heart today! Repent and commit it to God.

Day 2
Pray Psalms 51 in the first person tense for yourself, no matter who has hurt or betrayed you.

Day 3
Continue as an action of intent to forgive. Forgiveness is not a feeling -- but a commandment (to do). Release yourself from the torment, you deserve it. Pray "By faith (trust in God's ability) I choose to forgive those who have caused me pain in Jesus Name. I forgive name them as an act of faith.

Day 4
Begin thanking God for restoring your peace and for his forgiveness because you held onto unforgiveness in your heart!

Day 5
Wherefore my dearly beloved, flee from idolatry. (I Corinthians 10:13-14) Anything that occupies the space in our heart that belongs to God is idolatry.

Day 6
Could you be the one to share the gospel with them and save them from a burning hell! Remember one plants, another waters, and God gives the increase!

Day 7
What fruit can you pick from the Tree of Life to feed your heart today get started feeding the scriptures to your heart to manifest that fruit.

Week Thirty-Five: Good Heart
Reference: Weekly Plan Outline (See Appendix)

Every day tell yourself the truth, face that truth no matter how ugly it is, repent of it and commit it to God. This is an action not a feeling; you do it by faith continuously until you feel the release in your spirit or until it is no longer a chore but a pleasure!

What is a Good Heart?
beautiful, handsome, excellent, eminent, choice, surpassing, precious, useful, suitable, commendable, admirable, good, excellent in its nature and characteristics, and therefore well adapted to its ends, genuine, approved, precious, competent, able, such as one ought to be, praiseworthy, noble, praiseworthy, morally good, noble, honourable, conferring honour, affecting the mind agreeably, comforting and confirming

Hebrew: chaciyd khä ˈsed'
Greek: chrestotes khra-stoˈ-tas

Remember Jesus has proven himself faithful so that engrafted and adopted sons would receive the anointing to be faithful through his obedience to the Father.

Proverbs 14:14 ¹⁴ The backslider in heart shall be filled with his own ways: and a good man *shall be satisfied* from himself.

Hebrews 6:3-6 ³ And this will we do, if God permit. ⁴ For *it is* impossible for those who were once enlightened, and have tasted of the heavenly gift, and were made partakers of the Holy Ghost, ⁵ And have tasted the good word of God, and the powers of the world to come, ⁶ If they shall fall away, to renew them again unto repentance; seeing they crucify to themselves the Son of God afresh, and put *him* to an open shame.

Week Thirty-Five: Good Heart

Take comfort in the following passage(s):

Matthew 12:34-35 **34** O generation of vipers, how can ye, being evil, speak good things? for out of the abundance of the heart the mouth speaketh. **35** A good man out of the good treasure of the heart bringeth forth good things: and an evil man out of the evil treasure bringeth forth evil things.

Jeremiah 32:41 **41** Yea, I will rejoice over them to do them good, and I will plant them in this land assuredly with my whole heart and with my whole soul.

Philippians 4:8   Finally, brethren, whatsoever things are true, whatsoever things *are* honest, whatsoever things *are* just, whatsoever things *are* pure, whatsoever things *are* lovely, whatsoever things *are* of good report; if *there be* any virtue, and if *there be* any praise, think on these things.

What Weights and Burdens Come to Mind to Lay Down?

_____

_____

YOUR PERSONAL COMMITMENT TO GOD

Thanksgiving – Praise – Worship Your Way into His Presence
Opening Prayer (Remember Put on Your Armour!)
Scripture(s) Reading

Call to Action for the Day
Will I chose to believe the truth I've discovered?
Will I allow the truth to change my thinking and my conduct?
We must adjust ourselves to the Bible— never the Bible to ourselves.
Closing Prayer

Week Thirty-Five: Good Heart

GODS COMMITMENT TO YOU

Promises from the Father _____

_____

Priorities of the Day_____

_____

Benefits for the Day_____

_____

DECLARATIONS AND DECREES

Protection_____

_____

Strategies for the Day_____

_____

Week Thirty-Five: Good Heart
PRAISE REPORT

Cool of the Day Revelation_____

WEEK Thirty Six

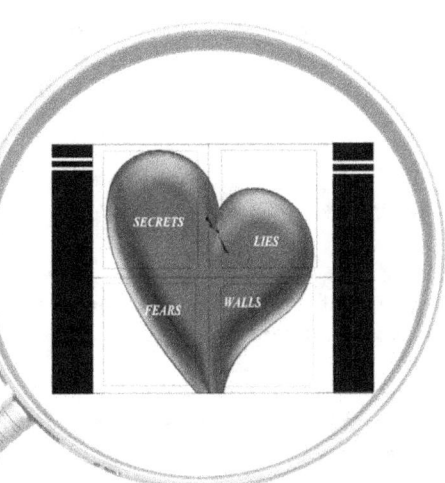

CALENDAR

Day		Sat	Sun	Mon	Tue	Wed	Thu	Fri
Date	Hour							
1st Watch	6–9 pm							
2nd Watch	9–12 am							
3rd Watch	12–3 am							
4th Watch	3–6 am							
5th Watch	6–9 am							
6th Watch	9–12 pm							
7th Watch	12–3 pm							
8th Watch	3–6 pm							

"...He will not forgive your transgressions nor your sins" (Joshua 24:19), that is to say, if we impenitently continue in them...."
Thomas Manton

Weekly Plan Synopsis *(See Appendix for full plan)*

Day 1
Telling yourself and God the truth about where you are in your heart today! Repent and commit it to God.

Day 2
Pray Psalms 51 in the first person tense for yourself, no matter who has hurt or betrayed you.

Day 3
Continue as an action of intent to forgive. Forgiveness is not a feeling -- but a commandment (to do). Release yourself from the torment, you deserve it. Pray "By faith (trust in God's ability) I choose to forgive those who have caused me pain in Jesus Name. I forgive name them as an act of faith.

Day 4
Begin thanking God for restoring your peace and for his forgiveness because you held onto unforgiveness in your heart!

Day 5
Wherefore my dearly beloved, flee from idolatry. (I Corinthians 10:13-14) Anything that occupies the space in our heart that belongs to God is idolatry.

Day 6
Could you be the one to share the gospel with them and save them from a burning hell! Remember one plants, another waters, and God gives the increase!

Day 7
What fruit can you pick from the Tree of Life to feed your heart today get started feeding the scriptures to your heart to manifest that fruit.

Week Thirty-Six: Overcharged Heart
Reference: Weekly Plan Outline (See Appendix)

Every day tell yourself the truth, face that truth no matter how ugly it is, repent of it and commit it to God. This is an action not a feeling; you do it by faith continuously until you feel the release in your spirit or until it is no longer a chore but a pleasure!

What is an Overcharged Heart?
to weigh down, overcharge

Greek: baryno

Remember Jesus has proven himself faithful so that engrafted and adopted sons would receive the anointing to be faithful through his obedience to the Father.

Luke 21:34-37 **34** And take heed to yourselves, lest at any time your hearts be overcharged with surfeiting, and drunkenness, and cares of this life, and *so* that day come upon you unawares. **35** For as a snare shall it come on all them that dwell on the face of the whole earth. **36** Watch ye therefore, and pray always, that ye may be accounted worthy to escape all these things that shall come to pass, and to stand before the Son of man. **3**

Isaiah 28:7-8 **7** But they also have erred through wine, and through strong drink are out of the way; the priest and the prophet have erred through strong drink, they are swallowed up of wine, they are out of the way through strong drink; they err in vision, they stumble *in* judgment. **8** For all tables are full of vomit *and* filthiness, *so that there is* no place *clean*.

Week Thirty-Six: Overcharged Heart

Take comfort in the following passage(s):
Isaiah 51:9-13 ⁹ Awake, awake, put on strength, O arm of the LORD; awake, as in the ancient days, in the generations of old. *Art* thou not it that hath cut Rahab, *and* wounded the dragon? ¹⁰ *Art* thou not it which hath dried the sea, the waters of the great deep; that hath made the depths of the sea a way for the ransomed to pass over? ¹¹ Therefore the redeemed of the LORD shall return, and come with singing unto Zion; and everlasting joy *shall be* upon their head: they shall obtain gladness and joy; *and* sorrow and mourning shall flee away. ¹² I, *even* I, *am* he that comforteth you: who *art* thou, that thou shouldest be afraid of a man *that* shall die, and of the son of man *which* shall be made *as* grass; ¹³ And forgettest the LORD thy maker, that hath stretched forth the heavens, and laid the foundations of the earth; and hast feared continually every day because of the fury of the oppressor, as if he were ready to destroy? and where *is* the fury of the oppressor?

What Weights and Burdens Come to Mind to Lay Down?

_____

_____

YOUR PERSONAL COMMITMENT TO GOD

Thanksgiving – Praise – Worship Your Way into His Presence
Opening Prayer (Remember Put on Your Armour!)
Scripture(s) Reading

Call to Action for the Day
Will I chose to believe the truth I've discovered?
Will I allow the truth to change my thinking and my conduct?
We must adjust ourselves to the Bible— never the Bible to ourselves.
Closing Prayer

Week Thirty-Six: Overcharged Heart

GODS COMMITMENT TO YOU

Promises from the Father _____

_____

Priorities of the Day_____

_____

Benefits for the Day_____

_____

DECLARATIONS AND DECREES

Protection_____

_____

Strategies for the Day_____

_____

Week Thirty-Six: Overcharged Heart

PRAISE REPORT

Cool of the Day Revelation_____

WEEK Thirty Seven

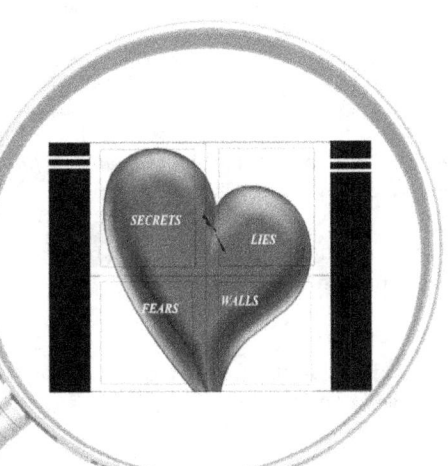

CALENDAR

Day	♥	Sat	Sun	Mon	Tue	Wed	Thu	Fri
Date	**Hour**							
1st Watch	6–9 pm							
2nd Watch	9–12 am							
3rd Watch	12–3 am							
4th Watch	3–6 am							
5th Watch	6–9 am							
6th Watch	9–12 pm							
7th Watch	12–3 pm							
8th Watch	3–6 pm							

> *"...Considering these things we receive the word with that trembling of heart which God so much respects..."*
> *Thomas Manton*

Weekly Plan Synopsis *(See Appendix for full plan)*

Day 1
Telling yourself and God the truth about where you are in your heart today! Repent and commit it to God.

Day 2
Pray Psalms 51 in the first person tense for yourself, no matter who has hurt or betrayed you.

Day 3
Continue as an action of intent to forgive. Forgiveness is not a feeling -- but a commandment (to do). Release yourself from the torment, you deserve it. Pray "By faith (trust in God's ability) I choose to forgive those who have caused me pain in Jesus Name. I forgive name them as an act of faith.

Day 4
Begin thanking God for restoring your peace and for his forgiveness because you held onto unforgiveness in your heart!

Day 5
Wherefore my dearly beloved, flee from idolatry. (I Corinthians 10:13-14) Anything that occupies the space in our heart that belongs to God is idolatry.

Day 6
Could you be the one to share the gospel with them and save them from a burning hell! Remember one plants, another waters, and God gives the increase!

Day 7
What fruit can you pick from the Tree of Life to feed your heart today get started feeding the scriptures to your heart to manifest that fruit.

Week Thirty-Seven: Troubled Heart

Reference: Weekly Plan Outline (See Appendix)

Every day tell yourself the truth, face that truth no matter how ugly it is, repent of it and commit it to God. This is an action not a feeling; you do it by faith continuously until you feel the release in your spirit or until it is no longer a chore but a pleasure!

What is a Troubled Heart?
to boil, foam, foam up, ferment, to be troubled, be in turmoil, to be reddened, to daub, seal up, cover or smear with asphalt

Hebrew: chamar

Remember Jesus has proven himself faithful so that engrafted and adopted sons would receive the anointing to be faithful through his obedience to the Father.

II Kings 6:11 [11] Therefore the heart of the king of Syria was sore troubled for this thing; and he called his servants, and said unto them, Will ye not shew me which of us *is* for the king of Israel?

Lamentations 1:20 Behold, O LORD; for I *am* in distress: my bowels are troubled; mine heart is turned within me; for I have grievously rebelled: abroad the sword bereaveth, at home *there is* as death.

Daniel 7:28 [28] Hitherto *is* the end of the matter. As for me Daniel, my cogitations much troubled me, and my countenance changed in me: but I kept the matter in my heart.

Week Thirty-Seven: Troubled Heart

Take comfort in the following passage(s):
John 14:1-3 ¹ Let not your heart be troubled: ye believe in God, believe also in me. ² In my Father's house are many mansions: if *it were* not *so*, I would have told you. I go to prepare a place for you. ³ And if I go and prepare a place for you, I will come again, and receive you unto myself; that where I am, *there* ye may be also.

John 14:27 ²⁷ Peace I leave with you, my peace I give unto you: not as the world giveth, give I unto you. Let not your heart be troubled, neither let it be afraid.

What Weights and Burdens Come to Mind to Lay Down?

_____

_____

YOUR PERSONAL COMMITMENT TO GOD

Thanksgiving – Praise – Worship Your Way into His Presence
Opening Prayer (Remember Put on Your Armour!)
Scripture(s) Reading

Call to Action for the Day
Will I chose to believe the truth I've discovered?
Will I allow the truth to change my thinking and my conduct?
We must adjust ourselves to the Bible— never the Bible to ourselves.
Closing Prayer

Week Thirty-Seven: Troubled Heart

GODS COMMITMENT TO YOU

Promises from the Father _____
_____

Priorities of the Day_____
_____

Benefits for the Day_____
_____

DECLARATIONS AND DECREES

Protection_____
_____

Strategies for the Day_____
_____

Week Thirty-Seven: Troubled Heart

PRAISE REPORT

Cool of the Day Revelation_____

WEEK Thirty Eight

CALENDAR

Day		Sat	Sun	Mon	Tue	Wed	Thu	Fri
Date	Hour							
1st Watch	6–9 pm							
2nd Watch	9–12 am							
3rd Watch	12–3 am							
4th Watch	3–6 am							
5th Watch	6–9 am							
6th Watch	9–12 pm							
7th Watch	12–3 pm							
8th Watch	3–6 pm							

"Every gracious soul stands in awe of the word of God,..."
Matthew Henry

Weekly Plan Synopsis *(See Appendix for full plan)*

Day 1
Telling yourself and God the truth about where you are in your heart today! Repent and commit it to God.

Day 2
Pray Psalms 51 in the first person tense for yourself, no matter who has hurt or betrayed you.

Day 3
Continue as an action of intent to forgive. Forgiveness is not a feeling -- but a commandment (to do). Release yourself from the torment, you deserve it. Pray "By faith (trust in God's ability) I choose to forgive those who have caused me pain in Jesus Name. I forgive name them as an act of faith.

Day 4
Begin thanking God for restoring your peace and for his forgiveness because you held onto unforgiveness in your heart!

Day 5
Wherefore my dearly beloved, flee from idolatry. (I Corinthians 10:13-14) Anything that occupies the space in our heart that belongs to God is idolatry.

Day 6
Could you be the one to share the gospel with them and save them from a burning hell! Remember one plants, another waters, and God gives the increase!

Day 7
What fruit can you pick from the Tree of Life to feed your heart today get started feeding the scriptures to your heart to manifest that fruit.

Week Thirty-Eight: Single Heart
Reference: Weekly Plan Outline (See Appendix)

Every day tell yourself the truth, face that truth no matter how ugly it is, repent of it and commit it to God. This is an action not a feeling; you do it by faith continuously until you feel the release in your spirit or until it is no longer a chore but a pleasure!

What is a Single Heart?
simple, single, whole, good fulfilling its office, sound, of the eye

Greek: haplous

Remember Jesus has proven himself faithful so that engrafted and adopted sons would receive the anointing to be faithful through his obedience to the Father.

Matthew 6:21-24 [21] For where your treasure is, there will your heart be also. [22] The light of the body is the eye: if therefore thine eye be single, thy whole body shall be full of light. [23] But if thine eye be evil, thy whole body shall be full of darkness. If therefore the light that is in thee be darkness, how great *is* that darkness! [24] No man can serve two masters: for either he will hate the one, and love the other; or else he will hold to the one, and despise the other. Ye cannot serve God and mammon.

Luke 11:34 [34] The light of the body is the eye: therefore when thine eye is single, thy whole body also is full of light; but when *thine eye* is evil, thy body also *is* full of darkness.

Week Thirty-Eight: Single Heart

Take comfort in the following passage(s):
1 Corinthians 3:16-21 [16] Know ye not that ye are the temple of God, and *that* the Spirit of God dwelleth in you? [17] If any man defile the temple of God, him shall God destroy; for the temple of God is holy, which *temple* ye are. [18] Let no man deceive himself. If any man among you seemeth to be wise in this world, let him become a fool, that he may be wise. [19] For the wisdom of this world is foolishness with God. For it is written, He taketh the wise in their own craftiness. [20] And again, The Lord knoweth the thoughts of the wise, that they are vain. [21] Therefore let no man glory in men.

What Weights and Burdens Come to Mind to Lay Down?

_____

_____

YOUR PERSONAL COMMITMENT TO GOD

Thanksgiving – Praise – Worship Your Way into His Presence
Opening Prayer (Remember Put on Your Armour!)
Scripture(s) Reading

Call to Action for the Day
Will I chose to believe the truth I've discovered?
Will I allow the truth to change my thinking and my conduct?
We must adjust ourselves to the Bible— never the Bible to ourselves.
Closing Prayer

Week Thirty-Eight: Single Heart: Broken Heart

GODS COMMITMENT TO YOU

Promises from the Father _____

_____

Priorities of the Day _____

_____

Benefits for the Day _____

_____

DECLARATIONS AND DECREES

Protection _____

_____

Strategies for the Day _____

_____

Week Thirty-Eight: Single Heart: Broken Heart
PRAISE REPORT

Cool of the Day Revelation_____

WEEK Thirty Nine

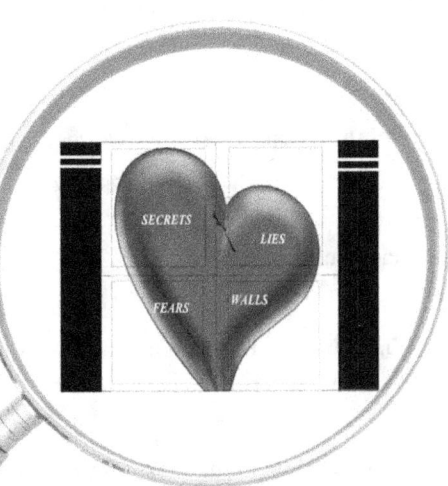

CALENDAR

Day		Sat	Sun	Mon	Tue	Wed	Thu	Fri
Date	Hour							
1st Watch	6–9 pm							
2nd Watch	9-12 am							
3rd Watch	12–3 am							
4th Watch	3–6 am							
5th Watch	6–9 am							
6th Watch	9–12 pm							
7th Watch	12–3 pm							
8th Watch	3–6 pm							

> *"...of the authority of its precepts and the terror of its threatenings;..."*
> Matthew Henry

Weekly Plan Synopsis *(See Appendix for full plan)*

Day 1
Telling yourself and God the truth about where you are in your heart today! Repent and commit it to God.

Day 2
Pray Psalms 51 in the first person tense for yourself, no matter who has hurt or betrayed you.

Day 3
Continue as an action of intent to forgive. Forgiveness is not a feeling -- but a commandment (to do). Release yourself from the torment, you deserve it. Pray "By faith (trust in God's ability) I choose to forgive those who have caused me pain in Jesus Name. I forgive name them as an act of faith.

Day 4
Begin thanking God for restoring your peace and for his forgiveness because you held onto unforgiveness in your heart!

Day 5
Wherefore my dearly beloved, flee from idolatry. (I Corinthians 10:13-14) Anything that occupies the space in our heart that belongs to God is idolatry.

Day 6
Could you be the one to share the gospel with them and save them from a burning hell! Remember one plants, another waters, and God gives the increase!

Day 7
What fruit can you pick from the Tree of Life to feed your heart today get started feeding the scriptures to your heart to manifest that fruit.

Week Thirty-Nine: Foolish Heart
Reference: Weekly Plan Outline (See Appendix)

Every day tell yourself the truth, face that truth no matter how ugly it is, repent of it and commit it to God. This is an action not a feeling; you do it by faith continuously until you feel the release in your spirit or until it is no longer a chore but a pleasure!

What is a Foolish Heart?
unintelligent, without understanding, stupid, fool, foolish, vile person, foolish man, foolish women

Hebrew: nabal nä vȧl'
Greek: asynetos ä-sü'-ne-tos

Remember Jesus has proven himself faithful so that engrafted and adopted sons would receive the anointing to be faithful through his obedience to the Father.

Romans 1:21-32 21 Because that, when they knew God, they glorified *him* not as God, neither were thankful; but became vain in their imaginations, and their foolish heart was darkened. 22 Professing themselves to be wise, they became fools, 23 And changed the glory of the uncorruptible God into an image made like to corruptible man, and to birds, and fourfooted beasts, and creeping things. 24 Wherefore God also gave them up to uncleanness through the lusts of their own hearts, to dishonour their own bodies between themselves: 25 Who changed the truth of God into a lie, and worshipped and served the creature more than the Creator, who is blessed for ever. Amen. 26 For this cause God gave them up unto vile affections: for even their women did change the natural use into that which is against nature: 27 And likewise also the men, leaving the natural use of the woman, burned in their lust one toward another; men with men working that which is unseemly, and receiving in themselves that recompence of their error which was meet. 28 And even as they did not like to retain God in *their* knowledge,

Week Thirty-Nine: Foolish Heart

God gave them over to a reprobate mind, to do those things which are not convenient; ²⁹ Being filled with all unrighteousness, fornication, wickedness, covetousness, maliciousness; full of envy, murder, debate, deceit, malignity; whisperers, ³⁰ Backbiters, haters of God, despiteful, proud, boasters, inventors of evil things, disobedient to parents, ³¹ Without understanding, covenant breakers, without natural affection, implacable, unmerciful: ³² Who knowing the judgment of God, that they which commit such things are worthy of death, not only do the same, but have pleasure in them that do them.

Take comfort in the following passage(s):

Proverbs 15:7 [7] The lips of the wise disperse knowledge: but the heart of the foolish *doeth* not so.

What Weights and Burdens Come to Mind to Lay Down?

_____

_____

YOUR PERSONAL COMMITMENT TO GOD

Thanksgiving – Praise – Worship Your Way into His Presence
Opening Prayer (Remember Put on Your Armour!)
Scripture(s) Reading

Call to Action for the Day
Will I chose to believe the truth I've discovered?
Will I allow the truth to change my thinking and my conduct?
We must adjust ourselves to the Bible— never the Bible to ourselves.
Closing Prayer

Week Thirty-Nine: Foolish Heart

GODS COMMITMENT TO YOU

Promises from the Father _____

_____

Priorities of the Day_____

_____

Benefits for the Day_____

_____

DECLARATIONS AND DECREES

Protection_____

_____

Strategies for the Day_____

_____

Week Thirty-Nine: Foolish Heart

PRAISE REPORT

Cool of the Day Revelation_____

WEEK Forty

CALENDAR

Day		Sat	Sun	Mon	Tue	Wed	Thu	Fri
Date	Hour							
1st Watch	6–9 pm							
2nd Watch	9–12 am							
3rd Watch	12–3 am							
4th Watch	3–6 am							
5th Watch	6–9 am							
6th Watch	9–12 pm							
7th Watch	12–3 pm							
8th Watch	3–6 pm							

"...and to those that do so nothing appears, in the power and wrath of man, at all formidable. We ought to obey God rather than men,..."
Matthew Henry

Weekly Plan Synopsis *(See Appendix for full plan)*

Day 1
Telling yourself and God the truth about where you are in your heart today! Repent and commit it to God.

Day 2
Pray Psalms 51 in the first person tense for yourself, no matter who has hurt or betrayed you.

Day 3
Continue as an action of intent to forgive. Forgiveness is not a feeling -- but a commandment (to do). Release yourself from the torment, you deserve it. Pray "By faith (trust in God's ability) I choose to forgive those who have caused me pain in Jesus Name. I forgive name them as an act of faith.

Day 4
Begin thanking God for restoring your peace and for his forgiveness because you held onto unforgiveness in your heart!

Day 5
Wherefore my dearly beloved, flee from idolatry. (I Corinthians 10:13-14) Anything that occupies the space in our heart that belongs to God is idolatry.

Day 6
Could you be the one to share the gospel with them and save them from a burning hell! Remember one plants, another waters, and God gives the increase!

Day 7
What fruit can you pick from the Tree of Life to feed your heart today get started feeding the scriptures to your heart to manifest that fruit.

Week Forty: Impenitent Heart
Reference: Weekly Plan Outline (See Appendix)

Every day tell yourself the truth, face that truth no matter how ugly it is, repent of it and commit it to God. This is an action not a feeling; you do it by faith continuously until you feel the release in your spirit or until it is no longer a chore but a pleasure!

What is an Impenitent Heart?
admitting no change of mind, unrepented, impenitent

Greek: ametanoetos

Remember Jesus has proven himself faithful so that engrafted and adopted sons would receive the anointing to be faithful through his obedience to the Father.

Romans 2:5-6 **5** But after thy hardness and impenitent heart treasurest ….the day of wrath and revelation of the righteous judgment of God; **6** Who will render to every man according to his deeds:

II Peter 2:10-22 **10** But chiefly them that walk after the flesh in the lust of uncleanness, and despise government. Presumptuous *are they*, selfwilled, they are not afraid to speak evil of dignities. **11** Whereas angels, which are greater in power and might, bring not railing accusation against them before the Lord. **12** But these, as natural brute beasts, made to be taken and destroyed, speak evil of the things that they understand not; and shall utterly perish in their own corruption; **13** And shall receive the reward of unrighteousness, *as* they that count it pleasure to riot in the day time. Spots *they are* and blemishes, sporting themselves with their own deceivings while they feast with you; **14** Having eyes full of adultery, and that cannot cease from sin; beguiling unstable souls: an heart they have exercised with covetous practices; cursed children: **15** Which have forsaken the right way, and are gone astray, following the way of Balaam *the son* of Bosor, who loved the wages of unrighteousness; **16** But was rebuked for his iniquity: the dumb

Week Forty: Impenitent Heart

ass speaking with man's voice forbad the madness of the prophet. [17] These are wells without water, clouds that are carried with a tempest; to whom the mist of darkness is reserved for ever. [18] For when they speak great swelling *words* of vanity, they allure through the lusts of the flesh, *through much* wantonness, those that were clean escaped from them who live in error. [19] While they promise them liberty, they themselves are the servants of corruption: for of whom a man is overcome, of the same is he brought in bondage. [20] For if after they have escaped the pollutions of the world through the knowledge of the Lord and Saviour Jesus Christ, they are again entangled therein, and overcome, the latter end is worse with them than the beginning. [21] For it had been better for them not to have known the way of righteousness, than, after they have known *it*, to turn from the holy commandment delivered unto them. [22] But it is happened unto them according to the true proverb, The dog *is* turned to his own vomit again; and the sow that was washed to her wallowing in the mire.

Take comfort in the following passage(s):
2 Peter 2:9 [9] The Lord knoweth how to deliver the godly out of temptations, and to reserve the unjust unto the day of judgment to be punished:

What Weights and Burdens Come to Mind to Lay Down?

_____

_____

YOUR PERSONAL COMMITMENT TO GOD
Thanksgiving – Praise – Worship Your Way into His Presence
Opening Prayer (Remember Put on Your Armour!)
Scripture(s) Reading
Call to Action for the Day
Will I chose to believe the truth I've discovered?
Will I allow the truth to change my thinking and my conduct?
We must adjust ourselves to the Bible— never the Bible to ourselves.
Closing Prayer

Week Forty: Impenitent Heart

GODS COMMITMENT TO YOU

Promises from the Father _____

_____

Priorities of the Day_____

_____

Benefits for the Day_____

_____

DECLARATIONS AND DECREES

Protection_____

_____

Strategies for the Day_____

_____

Week Forty: Impenitent Heart
PRAISE REPORT

Cool of the Day Revelation_____

WEEK Forty One

CALENDAR

Day	♥	Sat	Sun	Mon	Tue	Wed	Thu	Fri
Date	**Hour**							
1st Watch	6–9 pm							
2nd Watch	9-12 am							
3rd Watch	12–3 am							
4th Watch	3–6 am							
5th Watch	6–9 am							
6th Watch	9–12 pm							
7th Watch	12–3 pm							
8th Watch	3–6 pm							

"...and to make sure of God's favour,..."
Matthew Henry

Weekly Plan Synopsis *(See Appendix for full plan)*

Day 1
Telling yourself and God the truth about where you are in your heart today! Repent and commit it to God.

Day 2
Pray Psalms 51 in the first person tense for yourself, no matter who has hurt or betrayed you.

Day 3
Continue as an action of intent to forgive. Forgiveness is not a feeling -- but a commandment (to do). Release yourself from the torment, you deserve it. Pray "By faith (trust in God's ability) I choose to forgive those who have caused me pain in Jesus Name. I forgive name them as an act of faith.

Day 4
Begin thanking God for restoring your peace and for his forgiveness because you held onto unforgiveness in your heart!

Day 5
Wherefore my dearly beloved, flee from idolatry. (I Corinthians 10:13-14) Anything that occupies the space in our heart that belongs to God is idolatry.

Day 6
Could you be the one to share the gospel with them and save them from a burning hell! Remember one plants, another waters, and God gives the increase!

Day 7
What fruit can you pick from the Tree of Life to feed your heart today get started feeding the scriptures to your heart to manifest that fruit.

Week Forty-One: Circumcised Heart
Reference: Weekly Plan Outline (See Appendix)

Every day tell yourself the truth, face that truth no matter how ugly it is, repent of it and commit it to God. This is an action not a feeling; you do it by faith continuously until you feel the release in your spirit or until it is no longer a chore but a pleasure!

What is an Circumcised Heart?
since by the rite of circumcision a man was separated from the unclean world and dedicated to God, the word is transferred to denote the extinguishing of lusts and the removal of sins

Hebrew: peritome
Greek: peritemno

Remember Jesus has proven himself faithful so that engrafted and adopted sons would receive the anointing to be faithful through his obedience to the Father.

Colossians 2:11-15 [11] In whom also ye are circumcised with the circumcision made without hands, in putting off the body of the sins of the flesh by the circumcision of Christ: [12] Buried with him in baptism, wherein also ye are risen with *him* through the faith of the operation of God, who hath raised him from the dead. [13] And you, being dead in your sins and the uncircumcision of your flesh, hath he quickened together with him, having forgiven you all trespasses; [14] Blotting out the handwriting of ordinances that was against us, which was contrary to us, and took it out of the way, nailing it to his cross; [15] *And* having spoiled principalities and powers, he made a shew of them openly, triumphing over them in it.

Week Forty-One: Circumcised Heart

Take comfort in the following passage(s):

Philippians 1:27 [27] Only let your conversation be as it becometh the gospel of Christ: that whether I come and see you, or else be absent, I may hear of your affairs, that ye stand fast in one spirit, with one mind striving together for the faith of the gospel;

Because Paul's life had been radically transformed by the gospel, he was intent on living to honor the gospel that gave him life. It would have been tragic to receive the riches of the gospel and then to live as a spiritual pauper. It would have been disgraceful to be saved from death by the blood of Christ and then show no reverence for that sacrifice. It would have been foolish to accept such love from Christ and then to resent what He asked in return.

The way you live your life ought to be a tribute to the matchless grace that your Lord and Savior, Jesus Christ, has bestowed upon you.

—Experiencing God Day by Day

What Weights and Burdens Come to Mind to Lay Down?

_____

_____

YOUR PERSONAL COMMITMENT TO GOD
Thanksgiving – Praise – Worship Your Way into His Presence
Opening Prayer (Remember Put on Your Armour!)
Scripture(s) Reading

Call to Action for the Day
Will I chose to believe the truth I've discovered?
Will I allow the truth to change my thinking and my conduct?
We must adjust ourselves to the Bible— never the Bible to ourselves.
Closing Prayer

Week Forty-One: Circumcised Heart

GODS COMMITMENT TO YOU

Promises from the Father _____
_____

Priorities of the Day_____
_____

Benefits for the Day_____
_____

DECLARATIONS AND DECREES

Protection_____
_____

Strategies for the Day_____
_____

Week Forty-One: Circumcised Heart
PRAISE REPORT

Cool of the Day Revelation _____

WEEK Forty Two

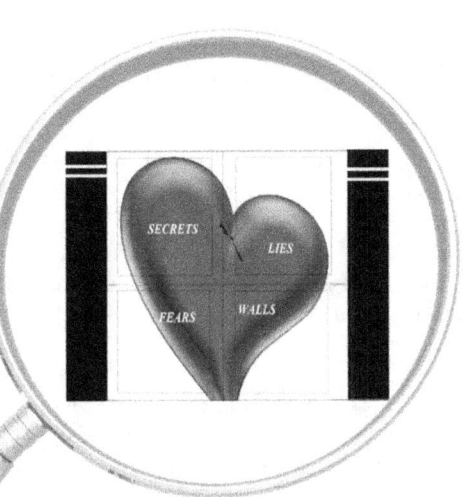

CALENDAR

Day		Sat	Sun	Mon	Tue	Wed	Thu	Fri
Date	Hour							
1st Watch	6–9 pm							
2nd Watch	9–12 am							
3rd Watch	12–3 am							
4th Watch	3–6 am							
5th Watch	6–9 am							
6th Watch	9–12 pm							
7th Watch	12–3 pm							
8th Watch	3–6 pm							

> *"...though we throw ourselves under the frowns of all the world,*
> *Luke 12:4- 5..."*
> *Matthew Henry*

Weekly Plan Synopsis *(See Appendix for full plan)*

Day 1
Telling yourself and God the truth about where you are in your heart today! Repent and commit it to God.

Day 2
Pray Psalms 51 in the first person tense for yourself, no matter who has hurt or betrayed you.

Day 3
Continue as an action of intent to forgive. Forgiveness is not a feeling -- but a commandment (to do). Release yourself from the torment, you deserve it. Pray "By faith (trust in God's ability) I choose to forgive those who have caused me pain in Jesus Name. I forgive name them as an act of faith.

Day 4
Begin thanking God for restoring your peace and for his forgiveness because you held onto unforgiveness in your heart!

Day 5
Wherefore my dearly beloved, flee from idolatry. (I Corinthians 10:13-14) Anything that occupies the space in our heart that belongs to God is idolatry.

Day 6
Could you be the one to share the gospel with them and save them from a burning hell! Remember one plants, another waters, and God gives the increase!

Day 7
What fruit can you pick from the Tree of Life to feed your heart today get started feeding the scriptures to your heart to manifest that fruit.

Week Forty-Two: Evil Heart
Reference: Weekly Plan Outline (See Appendix)

Every day tell yourself the truth, face that truth no matter how ugly it is, repent of it and commit it to God. This is an action not a feeling; you do it by faith continuously until you feel the release in your spirit or until it is no longer a chore but a pleasure!

What is an Evil Heart?
bad, disagreeable, malignant, unpleasant, displeasing, hurtful, unkind (vicious in disposition), injury, calamity, distress, adversity, wrong

Hebrew: ra'

Remember Jesus has proven himself faithful so that engrafted and adopted sons would receive the anointing to be faithful through his obedience to the Father.

Jeremiah 3:17 [17] At that time they shall call Jerusalem the throne of the LORD; and all the nations shall be gathered unto it, to the name of the LORD, to Jerusalem: neither shall they walk any more after the imagination of their evil heart.

Jeremiah 16:12-13 [12] And ye have done worse than your fathers; for, behold, ye walk every one after the imagination of his evil heart, that they may not hearken unto me: [13] Therefore will I cast you out of this land into a land that ye know not, *neither* ye nor your fathers; and there shall ye serve other gods day and night; where I will not shew you favour.

Week Forty-Two: Evil Heart

Take comfort in the following passage(s):
Hebrews 3:12-15 **12** Take heed, brethren, lest there be in any of you an evil heart of unbelief, in departing from the living God. **13** But exhort one another daily, while it is called To day; lest any of you be hardened through the deceitfulness of sin. **14** For we are made partakers of Christ, if we hold the beginning of our confidence stedfast unto the end; **15** While it is said, To day if ye will hear his voice, harden not your hearts, as in the provocation.

What Weights and Burdens Come to Mind to Lay Down?

_____

_____

YOUR PERSONAL COMMITMENT TO GOD

Thanksgiving – Praise – Worship Your Way into His Presence
Opening Prayer (Remember Put on Your Armour!)
Scripture(s) Reading

Call to Action for the Day
Will I chose to believe the truth I've discovered?
Will I allow the truth to change my thinking and my conduct?
We must adjust ourselves to the Bible— never the Bible to ourselves.
Closing Prayer

Week Forty-Two: Evil Heart

GODS COMMITMENT TO YOU

Promises from the Father _____

_____

Priorities of the Day_____

_____

Benefits for the Day_____

_____

DECLARATIONS AND DECREES

Protection_____

_____

Strategies for the Day_____

_____

Week Forty-Two: Evil Heart

PRAISE REPORT

Cool of the Day Revelation_____

_____

_____

_____

_____

_____

_____

_____

_____

_____

_____

_____

WEEK Forty Three

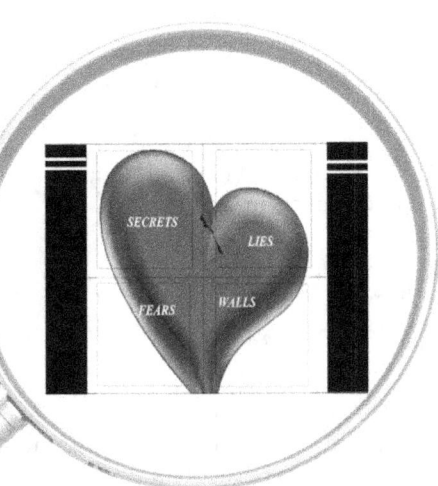

CALENDAR

Day	♥	Sat	Sun	Mon	Tue	Wed	Thu	Fri
Date	Hour							
1st Watch	6–9 pm							
2nd Watch	9–12 am							
3rd Watch	12–3 am							
4th Watch	3–6 am							
5th Watch	6–9 am							
6th Watch	9–12 pm							
7th Watch	12–3 pm							
8th Watch	3–6 pm							

"...The heart that stands in awe of God's word is armed against the temptations that arise from persecution..."
Matthew Henry

Weekly Plan Synopsis *(See Appendix for full plan)*

Day 1
Telling yourself and God the truth about where you are in your heart today! Repent and commit it to God.

Day 2
Pray Psalms 51 in the first person tense for yourself, no matter who has hurt or betrayed you.

Day 3
Continue as an action of intent to forgive. Forgiveness is not a feeling -- but a commandment (to do). Release yourself from the torment, you deserve it. Pray "By faith (trust in God's ability) I choose to forgive those who have caused me pain in Jesus Name. I forgive name them as an act of faith.

Day 4
Begin thanking God for restoring your peace and for his forgiveness because you held onto unforgiveness in your heart!

Day 5
Wherefore my dearly beloved, flee from idolatry. (I Corinthians 10:13-14) Anything that occupies the space in our heart that belongs to God is idolatry.

Day 6
Could you be the one to share the gospel with them and save them from a burning hell! Remember one plants, another waters, and God gives the increase!

Day 7
What fruit can you pick from the Tree of Life to feed your heart today get started feeding the scriptures to your heart to manifest that fruit.

Week Forty-Three: True Heart
Reference: Weekly Plan Outline (See Appendix)

Every day tell yourself the truth, face that truth no matter how ugly it is, repent of it and commit it to God. This is an action not a feeling; you do it by faith continuously until you feel the release in your spirit or until it is no longer a chore but a pleasure!

What is a True Heart?
that which has not only the name and resemblance, but the real nature corresponding to the name, in every respect corresponding to the idea signified by the name, real, true genuine, opposite to what is fictitious, counterfeit, imaginary, simulated or pretended, opposite to what is imperfect defective, frail, uncertain

Hebrew: 'emeth

Greek: alethinos

Remember Jesus has proven himself faithful so that engrafted and adopted sons would receive the anointing to be faithful through his obedience to the Father.

I Chronicles 12:32
³² And of the children of Issachar, *which were men* that had understanding of the times, to know what Israel ought to do; the heads of them *were* two hundred; and all their brethren *were* at their commandment.
Colossians 1:9-13 ⁹ For this cause we also, since the day we heard *it*, do not cease to pray for you, and to desire that ye might be filled with the knowledge of his will in all wisdom and spiritual understanding; ¹⁰ That ye might walk worthy of the Lord unto all pleasing, being fruitful in every good work, and increasing in the knowledge of God;
¹¹ Strengthened with all might, according to his glorious power, unto all patience and longsuffering with joyfulness;

Week Forty-Three: True Heart

¹² Giving thanks unto the Father, which hath made us meet to be partakers of the inheritance of the saints in light: [13] Who hath delivered us from the power of darkness, and hath translated *us* into the kingdom of his dear Son:

Take comfort in the following passage(s):

Hebrews 10:19-25 [19] Having therefore, brethren, boldness to enter into the holiest by the blood of Jesus, [20] By a new and living way, which he hath consecrated for us, through the veil, that is to say, his flesh; [21] And *having* an high priest over the house of God; [22] Let us draw near with a true heart in full assurance of faith, having our hearts sprinkled from an evil conscience, and our bodies washed with pure water. [23] Let us hold fast the profession of *our* faith without wavering; (for he *is* faithful that promised;) [24] And let us consider one another to provoke unto love and to good works: [25] Not forsaking the assembling of ourselves together, as the manner of some *is*; but exhorting *one another*: and so much the more, as ye see the day approaching.

What Weights and Burdens Come to Mind to Lay Down?

_____

_____

YOUR PERSONAL COMMITMENT TO GOD
Thanksgiving – Praise – Worship Your Way into His Presence
Opening Prayer (Remember Put on Your Armour!)
Scripture(s) Reading

Call to Action for the Day
Will I chose to believe the truth I've discovered?
Will I allow the truth to change my thinking and my conduct?
We must adjust ourselves to the Bible— never the Bible to ourselves.
Closing Prayer

Week Forty-Three: True Heart

GODS COMMITMENT TO YOU

Promises from the Father _____
_____

Priorities of the Day_____
_____

Benefits for the Day_____
_____

DECLARATIONS AND DECREES

Protection_____
_____

Strategies for the Day_____
_____

Week Forty-Three: True Heart
PRAISE REPORT

Cool of the Day Revelation_____

WEEK Forty Four

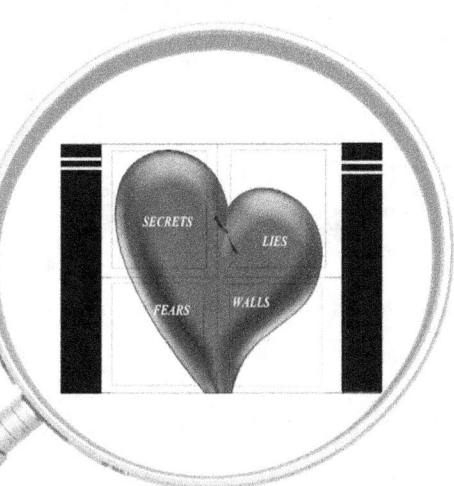

CALENDAR

Day		Sat	Sun	Mon	Tue	Wed	Thu	Fri
Date	Hour							
1st Watch	6–9 pm							
2nd Watch	9–12 am							
3rd Watch	12–3 am							
4th Watch	3–6 am							
5th Watch	6–9 am							
6th Watch	9–12 pm							
7th Watch	12–3 pm							
8th Watch	3–6 pm							

"Someone has well said that the Bible is like the ocean. You can wade in it, feed from it, live on it--or drown in it. But those who take the time to learn its truths and apply them will be changed forever."
Unknown

Weekly Plan Synopsis *(See Appendix for full plan)*

Day 1
Telling yourself and God the truth about where you are in your heart today! Repent and commit it to God.

Day 2
Pray Psalms 51 in the first person tense for yourself, no matter who has hurt or betrayed you.

Day 3
Continue as an action of intent to forgive. Forgiveness is not a feeling -- but a commandment (to do). Release yourself from the torment, you deserve it. Pray "By faith (trust in God's ability) I choose to forgive those who have caused me pain in Jesus Name. I forgive name them as an act of faith.

Day 4
Begin thanking God for restoring your peace and for his forgiveness because you held onto unforgiveness in your heart!

Day 5
Wherefore my dearly beloved, flee from idolatry. (I Corinthians 10:13-14) Anything that occupies the space in our heart that belongs to God is idolatry.

Day 6
Could you be the one to share the gospel with them and save them from a burning hell! Remember one plants, another waters, and God gives the increase!

Day 7
What fruit can you pick from the Tree of Life to feed your heart today get started feeding the scriptures to your heart to manifest that fruit.

Week Forty-Four: Hard Heart
Reference: Weekly Plan Outline (See Appendix)

Every day tell yourself the truth, face that truth no matter how ugly it is, repent of it and commit it to God. This is an action not a feeling; you do it by faith continuously until you feel the release in your spirit or until it is no longer a chore but a pleasure!

What is a Hard Heart?
great, grievous, heavy, sore, hard, much, slow, hardened, heavier, laden, thick ,hard, fierce

Hebrew: kabed
Greek: skleros

Remember Jesus has proven himself faithful so that engrafted and adopted sons would receive the anointing to be faithful through his obedience to the Father.

II Chronicles 9:1-2 **1** And when the queen of Sheba heard of the fame of Solomon, she came to prove Solomon with hard questions at Jerusalem, with a very great company, and camels that bare spices, and gold in abundance, and precious stones: and when she was come to Solomon, she communed with him of all that was in her heart. **2** And Solomon told her all her questions: and there was nothing hid from Solomon which he told her not.

Job 41:24-34 **24** His heart is as firm as a stone; yea, as hard as a piece of the nether *millstone*. **25** When he raiseth up himself, the mighty are afraid: by reason of breakings they purify themselves. **26** The sword of him that layeth at him cannot hold: the spear, the dart, nor the habergeon. **27** He esteemeth iron as straw, *and* brass as rotten wood. **28** The arrow cannot make him flee: slingstones are turned with him into stubble. **29** Darts are counted as stubble: he laugheth at the shaking of a spear. **30** Sharp

Week Forty-Four: Hard Heart

stones *are* under him: he spreadeth sharp pointed things upon the mire. ³¹ He maketh the deep to boil like a pot: he maketh the sea like a pot of ointment. ³² He maketh a path to shine after him; *one* would think the deep *to be* hoary. ³³ Upon earth there is not his like, who is made without fear. ³⁴ He beholdeth all high *things*: he *is* a king over all the children of pride.

Take comfort in the following passage(s):
Psalms 69:13-21 ¹³ "But as for me, my prayer *is* unto thee, O LORD, *in* an acceptable time: O God, in the multitude of thy mercy hear me, in the truth of thy salvation. ¹⁴ Deliver me out of the mire, and let me not sink: let me be delivered from them that hate me, and out of the deep waters. ¹⁵ Let not the waterflood overflow me, neither let the deep swallow me up, and let not the pit shut her mouth upon me. ¹⁶ Hear me, O LORD; for thy lovingkindness *is* good: turn unto me according to the multitude of thy tender mercies. ¹⁷ And hide not thy face from thy servant; for I am in trouble: hear me speedily. ¹⁸ Draw nigh unto my soul, *and* redeem it: deliver me because of mine enemies…"

What Weights and Burdens Come to Mind to Lay Down?

_____

_____

YOUR PERSONAL COMMITMENT TO GOD
Thanksgiving – Praise – Worship Your Way into His Presence
Opening Prayer (Remember Put on Your Armour!)
Scripture(s) Reading
Call to Action for the Day
Will I chose to believe the truth I've discovered?
Will I allow the truth to change my thinking and my conduct?
We must adjust ourselves to the Bible— never the Bible to ourselves.
Closing Prayer

Week Forty-Four: Hard Heart

GODS COMMITMENT TO YOU

Promises from the Father _____

_____

Priorities of the Day_____

_____

Benefits for the Day_____

_____

DECLARATIONS AND DECREES

Protection_____

_____

Strategies for the Day_____

_____

Week Forty-Four: Hard Heart
PRAISE REPORT

Cool of the Day Revelation_____

WEEK Forty Five

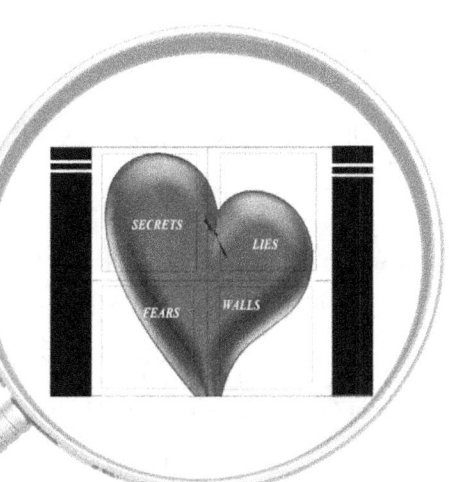

CALENDAR

Day		Sat	Sun	Mon	Tue	Wed	Thu	Fri
Date	Hour							
1st Watch	6–9 pm							
2nd Watch	9–12 am							
3rd Watch	12–3 am							
4th Watch	3–6 am							
5th Watch	6–9 am							
6th Watch	9–12 pm							
7th Watch	12–3 pm							
8th Watch	3–6 pm							

A Bible that is falling apart usually belongs to someone who isn't!
Unknown

Weekly Plan Synopsis *(See Appendix for full plan)*

Day 1
Telling yourself and God the truth about where you are in your heart today! Repent and commit it to God.

Day 2
Pray Psalms 51 in the first person tense for yourself, no matter who has hurt or betrayed you.

Day 3
Continue as an action of intent to forgive. Forgiveness is not a feeling -- but a commandment (to do). Release yourself from the torment, you deserve it. Pray "By faith (trust in God's ability) I choose to forgive those who have caused me pain in Jesus Name. I forgive name them as an act of faith.

Day 4
Begin thanking God for restoring your peace and for his forgiveness because you held onto unforgiveness in your heart!

Day 5
Wherefore my dearly beloved, flee from idolatry. (I Corinthians 10:13-14) Anything that occupies the space in our heart that belongs to God is idolatry.

Day 6
Could you be the one to share the gospel with them and save them from a burning hell! Remember one plants, another waters, and God gives the increase!

Day 7
What fruit can you pick from the Tree of Life to feed your heart today get started feeding the scriptures to your heart to manifest that fruit.

Week Forty-Five: Non-Perceiving Heart
Reference: Weekly Plan Outline (See Appendix)

Every day tell yourself the truth, face that truth no matter how ugly it is, repent of it and commit it to God. This is an action not a feeling; you do it by faith continuously until you feel the release in your spirit or until it is no longer a chore but a pleasure!

What is a Non-Perceiving Heart?
Void of understanding, dull of hearing and sight, refusing to understand

Remember Jesus has proven himself faithful so that engrafted and adopted sons would receive the anointing to be faithful through his obedience to the Father.

Deuteronomy 29:3-4 The great temptations which thine eyes have seen, the signs, and those great miracles: 4 Yet the LORD hath not given you an heart to perceive, and eyes to see, and ears to hear, unto this day.

Isaiah 6:9 9 And he said, Go, and tell this people, Hear ye indeed, but understand

Romans 11:7-8 What then? Israel hath not obtained that which he seeketh for; but the election hath obtained it, and the rest were blinded 8 (According as it is written, God hath given them the spirit of slumber, eyes that they should not see, and ears that they should not hear;) unto this day.

II Kings 17:34-35 Unto this day they do after the former manners: they fear not the LORD, neither do they after their statutes, or after their ordinances, or after the law and commandment which the LORD commanded the children of Jacob, whom he named Israel; 35 With whom the LORD had made a covenant, and charged them, saying, Ye shall not fear other gods, nor bow yourselves to them, nor serve them, nor sacrifice to them:

Week Forty-Five: Non-Perceiving Heart

Take comfort in the following passage(s):

Matthew 6:32-34 **32** (For after all these things do the Gentiles seek:) for your heavenly Father knoweth that ye have need of all these things. **33** But seek ye first the kingdom of God, and his righteousness; and all these things shall be added unto you. **34** Take therefore no thought for the morrow: for the morrow shall take thought for the things of itself. Sufficient unto the day *is* the evil thereof.

Matthew 10:28-29 **28** And fear not them which kill the body, but are not able to kill the soul: but rather fear him which is able to destroy both soul and body in hell. **29** Are not two sparrows sold for a farthing? and one of them shall not fall on the ground without your Father.

What Weights and Burdens Come to Mind to Lay Down?

_____

_____

YOUR PERSONAL COMMITMENT TO GOD

Thanksgiving – Praise – Worship Your Way into His Presence
Opening Prayer (Remember Put on Your Armour!)
Scripture(s) Reading

Call to Action for the Day
Will I chose to believe the truth I've discovered?
Will I allow the truth to change my thinking and my conduct?
We must adjust ourselves to the Bible— never the Bible to ourselves.
Closing Prayer

Week Forty-Five: Non-Perceiving Heart

GODS COMMITMENT TO YOU

Promises from the Father _____

_____

Priorities of the Day_____

_____

Benefits for the Day_____

_____

DECLARATIONS AND DECREES

Protection_____

_____

Strategies for the Day_____

_____

Week Forty-Five: Non-Perceiving Heart
PRAISE REPORT

Cool of the Day Revelation_____

WEEK Forty Six

CALENDAR

Day	♥	Sat	Sun	Mon	Tue	Wed	Thu	Fri
Date	**Hour**							
1st Watch	6–9 pm							
2nd Watch	9-12 am							
3rd Watch	12–3 am							
4th Watch	3–6 am							
5th Watch	6–9 am							
6th Watch	9–12 pm							
7th Watch	12–3 pm							
8th Watch	3–6 pm							

> *"If your life depended on knowing the Bible, how long would you live? We must approach God's Word as if our life depends on it--because it does."*
> Unknown

Weekly Plan Synopsis *(See Appendix for full plan)*

Day 1
Telling yourself and God the truth about where you are in your heart today! Repent and commit it to God.

Day 2
Pray Psalms 51 in the first person tense for yourself, no matter who has hurt or betrayed you.

Day 3
Continue as an action of intent to forgive. Forgiveness is not a feeling -- but a commandment (to do). Release yourself from the torment, you deserve it. Pray "By faith (trust in God's ability) I choose to forgive those who have caused me pain in Jesus Name. I forgive name them as an act of faith.

Day 4
Begin thanking God for restoring your peace and for his forgiveness because you held onto unforgiveness in your heart!

Day 5
Wherefore my dearly beloved, flee from idolatry. (I Corinthians 10:13-14) Anything that occupies the space in our heart that belongs to God is idolatry.

Day 6
Could you be the one to share the gospel with them and save them from a burning hell! Remember one plants, another waters, and God gives the increase!

Day 7
What fruit can you pick from the Tree of Life to feed your heart today get started feeding the scriptures to your heart to manifest that fruit.

Week Forty-Six: Whorish Heart
Reference: Weekly Plan Outline (See Appendix)

Every day tell yourself the truth, face that truth no matter how ugly it is, repent of it and commit it to God...

What is a Whorish Heart?
Figuratively - to be unfaithful to God
harlot, go a whoring, ...whoredom, whore, commit fornication, whorish, harlot, commit, continually, great, whore's, or cause to commit adultery, to cause to commit adultery, to be a cult prostitute

Hebrew: zanah

Remember Jesus has proven himself faithful so that engrafted and adopted sons would receive the anointing to be faithful through his obedience to the Father.

Ezekiel 6:8-10 ⁸ Yet will I leave a remnant, that ye may have *some* that shall escape the sword among the nations, when ye shall be scattered through the countries. ⁹ And they that escape of you shall remember me among the nations whither they shall be carried captives, because I am broken with their whorish heart, which hath departed from me, and with their eyes, which go a whoring after their idols: and they shall lothe themselves for the evils which they have committed in all their abominations. ¹⁰ And they shall know that I *am* the LORD, *and that* I have not said in vain that I would do this evil unto them.

Ezekiel 16:30-34 ³⁰ How weak is thine heart, saith the Lord GOD, seeing thou doest all these *things*, the work of an imperious whorish woman; ³¹ In that thou buildest thine eminent place in the head of every way, and makest thine high place in every street; and hast not been as an harlot, in that thou scornest hire; ³² *But as* a wife that committeth adultery, *which* taketh strangers instead of her husband!

Week Forty-Six: Whorish Heart

[33] They give gifts to all whores: but thou givest thy gifts to all thy lovers, and hirest them, that they may come unto thee on every side for thy whoredom. [34] And the contrary is in thee from *other* women in thy whoredoms, whereas none followeth thee to commit whoredoms: and in that thou givest a reward, and no reward is given unto thee, therefore thou art contrary.

Take comfort in the following passage(s):
Hebrews 7:11,12,15,16-22-... another priest should rise after the order of Melchisedec, and not be called after the order of Aaron? [12] For the priesthood being changed, there is made of necessity a change also of the law...[15] And it is yet far more evident: for that after the similitude of Melchisedec there ariseth another priest, [16] Who is made, not after the law of a carnal commandment, but after the power of an endless life. [17] For he testifieth, Thou *art* a priest for ever after the order of Melchisedec. [1]...The Lord sware and will not repent, Thou *art* a priest for ever after the order of Melchisedec:) [22] By so much was Jesus made a surety of a better testament..... [25] Wherefore he is able also to save them to the uttermost that come unto God by him, seeing he ever liveth to make intercession for them."

What Weights and Burdens Come to Mind to Lay Down?

_____

_____

YOUR PERSONAL COMMITMENT TO GOD
Thanksgiving – Praise – Worship Your Way into His Presence
Opening Prayer (Remember Put on Your Armour!)
Scripture(s) Reading
Call to Action for the Day
Will I chose to believe the truth I've discovered?
Will I allow the truth to change my thinking and my conduct?
We must adjust ourselves to the Bible— never the Bible to ourselves.
Closing Prayer

Week Forty-Six: Whorish Heart

GODS COMMITMENT TO YOU

Promises from the Father _____

_____

Priorities of the Day_____

_____

Benefits for the Day_____

_____

DECLARATIONS AND DECREES

Protection_____

_____

Strategies for the Day_____

_____

Week Forty-Six: Whorish Heart

PRAISE REPORT

Cool of the Day Revelation_____

WEEK Forty Seven

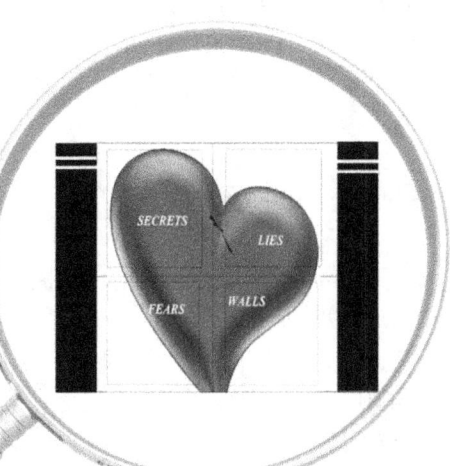

CALENDAR

Day	♥	Sat	Sun	Mon	Tue	Wed	Thu	Fri
Date	**Hour**							
1st Watch	6–9 pm							
2nd Watch	9-12 am							
3rd Watch	12–3 am							
4th Watch	3–6 am							
5th Watch	6–9 am							
6th Watch	9–12 pm							
7th Watch	12–3 pm							
8th Watch	3–6 pm							

"Someone has well said that the Bible is like the ocean. You can wade in it, feed from it, live on it--or drown in it. But those who take the time to learn its truths and apply them will be changed forever."
Unknown

Weekly Plan Synopsis *(See Appendix for full plan)*

Day 1
Telling yourself and God the truth about where you are in your heart today! Repent and commit it to God.

Day 2
Pray Psalms 51 in the first person tense for yourself, no matter who has hurt or betrayed you.

Day 3
Continue as an action of intent to forgive. Forgiveness is not a feeling -- but a commandment (to do). Release yourself from the torment, you deserve it. Pray "By faith (trust in God's ability) I choose to forgive those who have caused me pain in Jesus Name. I forgive name them as an act of faith.

Day 4
Begin thanking God for restoring your peace and for his forgiveness because you held onto unforgiveness in your heart!

Day 5
Wherefore my dearly beloved, flee from idolatry. (I Corinthians 10:13-14) Anything that occupies the space in our heart that belongs to God is idolatry.

Day 6
Could you be the one to share the gospel with them and save them from a burning hell! Remember one plants, another waters, and God gives the increase!

Day 7
What fruit can you pick from the Tree of Life to feed your heart today get started feeding the scriptures to your heart to manifest that fruit.

Week Forty-Seven: Mischievous Heart
Reference: Weekly Plan Outline (See Appendix)

Every day tell yourself the truth, face that truth no matter how ugly it is, repent of it and commit it to God. This is an action not a feeling; you do it by faith continuously until you feel the release in your spirit or until it is no longer a chore but a pleasure!

What is a Mischievous Heart?
desire in bad sense, chasm (figurative of destruction), engulfing ruin, calamity, disagreeable, malignant, unpleasant, evil (giving pain

Hebrew: havvah
Greek: ra`

Remember Jesus has proven himself faithful so that engrafted and adopted sons would receive the anointing to be faithful through his obedience to the Father.

Psalms 21:11-12 [11] For they intended evil against thee: they imagined a mischievous device, *which* they are not able *to perform.* [12] Therefore shalt thou make them turn their back, *when* thou shalt make ready *thine arrows* upon thy strings against the face of them.

Psalms 38:12 [12] They also that seek after my life lay snares *for me*: and they that seek my hurt speak mischievous things, and imagine deceits all the day long

Proverbs 24:8-9 [8] He that deviseth to do evil shall be called a mischievous person. [9] The thought of foolishness *is* sin: and the scorner *is* an abomination to men.

Ecclesiastes 10:13 [13] The beginning of the words of his mouth *is* foolishness: and the end of his talk *is* mischievous madness

Week Forty-Seven: Mischievous Heart

Take comfort in the following passage(s):
I Corinthians 4:5-6 **5** Therefore judge nothing before the time, until the Lord come, who both will bring to light the hidden things of darkness, and will make manifest the counsels of the hearts: and then shall every man have praise of God. **6** And these things, brethren, I have in a figure transferred to myself and *to* Apollos for your sakes; that ye might learn in us not to think *of men* above that which is written, that no one of you be puffed up for one against another.

Colossians 2:18 **18** Let no man beguile you of your reward in a voluntary humility and worshipping of angels, intruding into those things which he hath not seen, vainly puffed up by his fleshly mind,

What Weights and Burdens Come to Mind to Lay Down?

_____

_____

YOUR PERSONAL COMMITMENT TO GOD

Thanksgiving – Praise – Worship Your Way into His Presence
Opening Prayer (Remember Put on Your Armour!)
Scripture(s) Reading

Call to Action for the Day
Will I chose to believe the truth I've discovered?
Will I allow the truth to change my thinking and my conduct?
We must adjust ourselves to the Bible— never the Bible to ourselves.
Closing Prayer

Week Forty-Seven: Mischievous Heart

GODS COMMITMENT TO YOU

Promises from the Father _____
_____

Priorities of the Day_____
_____

Benefits for the Day_____
_____

DECLARATIONS AND DECREES

Protection_____
_____

Strategies for the Day_____
_____

Week Forty-Seven: Mischievous Heart

PRAISE REPORT

Cool of the Day Revelation_____

WEEK Forty Eight

CALENDAR

Day		Sat	Sun	Mon	Tue	Wed	Thu	Fri
Date	**Hour**							
1st Watch	6–9 pm							
2nd Watch	9–12 am							
3rd Watch	12–3 am							
4th Watch	3–6 am							
5th Watch	6–9 am							
6th Watch	9–12 pm							
7th Watch	12–3 pm							
8th Watch	3–6 pm							

Apply yourself to the whole text, and apply the whole text to yourself.
J. A. Bengel

Weekly Plan Synopsis *(See Appendix for full plan)*

Day 1
Telling yourself and God the truth about where you are in your heart today! Repent and commit it to God.

Day 2
Pray Psalms 51 in the first person tense for yourself, no matter who has hurt or betrayed you.

Day 3
Continue as an action of intent to forgive. Forgiveness is not a feeling -- but a commandment (to do). Release yourself from the torment, you deserve it. Pray "By faith (trust in God's ability) I choose to forgive those who have caused me pain in Jesus Name. I forgive name them as an act of faith.

Day 4
Begin thanking God for restoring your peace and for his forgiveness because you held onto unforgiveness in your heart!

Day 5
Wherefore my dearly beloved, flee from idolatry. (I Corinthians 10:13-14) Anything that occupies the space in our heart that belongs to God is idolatry.

Day 6
Could you be the one to share the gospel with them and save them from a burning hell! Remember one plants, another waters, and God gives the increase!

Day 7
What fruit can you pick from the Tree of Life to feed your heart today get started feeding the scriptures to your heart to manifest that fruit.

Week Forty-Eight: Living Heart
Reference: Weekly Plan Outline (See Appendix)

Every day tell yourself the truth, face that truth no matter how ugly it is, repent of it and commit it to God. This is an action not a feeling; you do it by faith continuously until you feel the release in your spirit or until it is no longer a chore but a pleasure!

What is a Living Heart?
living, alive, flowing, active (of man), reviving (of the springtime), life, sustenance, maintenance, revival, renewal, community and Metaphorically to be in full vigour, to be fresh, strong, efficient, powerful, efficacious, to live, breathe, be among the living (not lifeless, not dead), to enjoy real life, to have true life and worthy of the name, blessed, endless in the kingdom of God, living water, having vital power in itself and exerting the same upon the soul

Hebrew: chay
Greek: zao

Remember Jesus has proven himself faithful so that engrafted and adopted sons would receive the anointing to be faithful through his obedience to the Father.

Genesis 8:21-22 [21] And the LORD smelled a sweet savour; and the LORD said in his heart, I will not again curse the ground any more for man's sake; for the imagination of man's heart *is* evil from his youth; neither will I again smite any more every thing living, as I have done. [22] While the earth remaineth, seedtime and harvest, and cold and heat, and summer and winter, and day and night shall not cease.

Week Forty-Eight: Living Heart

Take comfort in the following passage(s):
Hebrews 3:12-15 [12] Take heed, brethren, lest there be in any of you an evil heart of unbelief, in departing from the living God. [13] But exhort one another daily, while it is called To day; lest any of you be hardened through the deceitfulness of sin. [14] For we are made partakers of Christ, if we hold the beginning of our confidence stedfast unto the end; [15] While it is said, To day if ye will hear his voice, harden not your hearts, as in the provocation.

II Corinthians 3:3-5 [3] *Forasmuch as ye are* manifestly declared to be the epistle of Christ ministered by us, written not with ink, but with the Spirit of the living God; not in tables of stone, but in fleshy tables of the heart. [4] And such trust have we through Christ to God-ward: [5] Not that we are sufficient of ourselves to think any thing as of ourselves; but our sufficiency *is* of God;

What Weights and Burdens Come to Mind to Lay Down?

_____

_____

YOUR PERSONAL COMMITMENT TO GOD

Thanksgiving – Praise – Worship Your Way into His Presence
Opening Prayer (Remember Put on Your Armour!)
Scripture(s) Reading

Call to Action for the Day
Will I chose to believe the truth I've discovered?
Will I allow the truth to change my thinking and my conduct?
We must adjust ourselves to the Bible— never the Bible to ourselves.
Closing Prayer

Week Forty-Eight: Living Heart

GODS COMMITMENT TO YOU

Promises from the Father _____

_____

Priorities of the Day_____

_____

Benefits for the Day_____

_____

DECLARATIONS AND DECREES

Protection_____

_____

Strategies for the Day_____

_____

Week Forty-Eight: Living Heart
PRAISE REPORT

Cool of the Day Revelation_____

WEEK Forty Nine

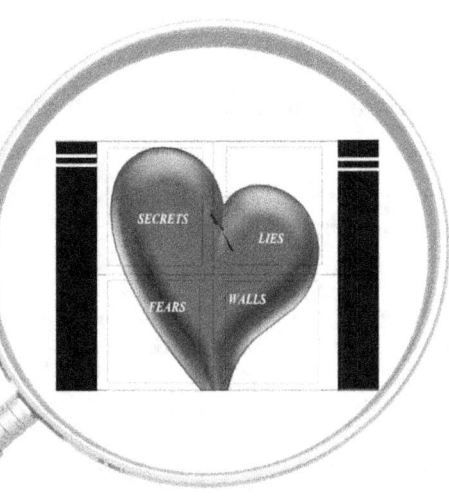

CALENDAR

Day		Sat	Sun	Mon	Tue	Wed	Thu	Fri
Date	Hour							
1st Watch	6–9 pm							
2nd Watch	9-12 am							
3rd Watch	12–3 am							
4th Watch	3–6 am							
5th Watch	6–9 am							
6th Watch	9–12 pm							
7th Watch	12–3 pm							
8th Watch	3–6 pm							

> *"As we search the Scriptures, we must allow them to search us, to sit in judgement upon our character and conduct."*
> Jerry Bridges

Weekly Plan Synopsis *(See Appendix for full plan)*

Day 1
Telling yourself and God the truth about where you are in your heart today! Repent and commit it to God.

Day 2
Pray Psalms 51 in the first person tense for yourself, no matter who has hurt or betrayed you.

Day 3
Continue as an action of intent to forgive. Forgiveness is not a feeling -- but a commandment (to do). Release yourself from the torment, you deserve it. Pray "By faith (trust in God's ability) I choose to forgive those who have caused me pain in Jesus Name. I forgive name them as an act of faith.

Day 4
Begin thanking God for restoring your peace and for his forgiveness because you held onto unforgiveness in your heart!

Day 5
Wherefore my dearly beloved, flee from idolatry. (I Corinthians 10:13-14) Anything that occupies the space in our heart that belongs to God is idolatry.

Day 6
Could you be the one to share the gospel with them and save them from a burning hell! Remember one plants, another waters, and God gives the increase!

Day 7
What fruit can you pick from the Tree of Life to feed your heart today get started feeding the scriptures to your heart to manifest that fruit.

Week Forty-Nine: Understanding Heart
Reference: Weekly Plan Outline (See Appendix)

Every day tell yourself the truth, face that truth no matter how ugly it is, repent of it and commit it to God. This is an action not a feeling; you do it by faith continuously until you feel the release in your spirit or until it is no longer a chore but a pleasure!

What is a Understanding Heart?
to hear, listen to, obey, perceive by ear, to hear of or concerning, o hear (have power to hear), to hear with attention or interest, listen to, to understand (language), to listen, give heed and to discern, understand, consider, know (with the mind), to observe, mark, give heed to, distinguish, consider, to have discernment, insight, understanding, to teach or instruct, to obey, be obedient, to make proclamation, summon

Hebrew: shama`
Greek: biyn

Remember Jesus has proven himself faithful so that engrafted and adopted sons would receive the anointing to be faithful through his obedience to the Father.

Hebrews 10:19-24 [19] Having therefore, brethren, boldness to enter into the holiest by the blood of Jesus, [20] By a new and living way, which he hath consecrated for us, through the veil, that is to say, his flesh; [21] And *having* an high priest over the house of God; [22] Let us draw near with a true heart in full assurance of faith, having our hearts sprinkled from an evil conscience, and our bodies washed with pure water. [23] Let us hold fast the profession of *our* faith without wavering; (for he *is* faithful that promised;) [24] And let us consider one another to provoke unto love and to good works:

Week Forty-Nine: Understanding Heart

Take comfort in the following passage(s):

Isaiah 11:1-3 **1** And there shall come forth a rod out of the stem of Jesse, and a Branch shall grow out of his roots: **2** And the spirit of the LORD shall rest upon him, the spirit of wisdom and understanding, the spirit of counsel and might, the spirit of knowledge and of the fear of the LORD; **3** And shall make him of quick understanding in the fear of the LORD: and he shall not judge after the sight of his eyes, neither reprove after the hearing of his ears:

I Thessalonians 5:11-13 **11** Wherefore comfort yourselves together, and edify one another, even as also ye do. **12** And we beseech you, brethren, to know them which labour among you, and are over you in the Lord, and admonish you; **13** And to esteem them very highly in love for their work's sake. *And* be at peace among yourselves.

What Weights and Burdens Come to Mind to Lay Down?

_____

_____

YOUR PERSONAL COMMITMENT TO GOD

Thanksgiving – Praise – Worship Your Way into His Presence
Opening Prayer (Remember Put on Your Armour!)
Scripture(s) Reading

Call to Action for the Day
Will I chose to believe the truth I've discovered?
Will I allow the truth to change my thinking and my conduct?
We must adjust ourselves to the Bible— never the Bible to ourselves.
Closing Prayer

Week Forty-Nine Living Heart

GODS COMMITMENT TO YOU

Promises from the Father _____

_____

Priorities of the Day_____

_____

Benefits for the Day_____

_____

DECLARATIONS AND DECREES

Protection_____

_____

Strategies for the Day_____

_____

Week Forty-Nine Living Heart

PRAISE REPORT

Cool of the Day Revelation_____

WEEK Fifty

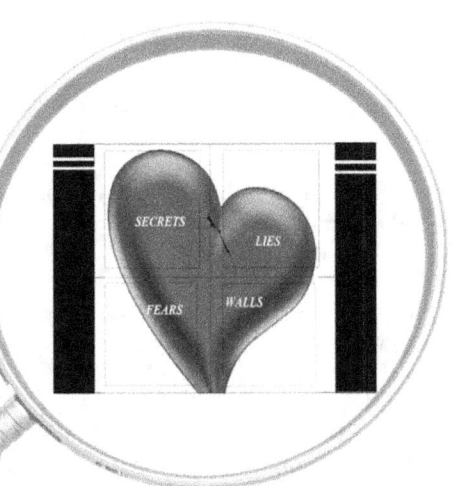

CALENDAR

Day	♥	Sat	Sun	Mon	Tue	Wed	Thu	Fri
Date	**Hour**							
1st Watch	6–9 pm							
2nd Watch	9-12 am							
3rd Watch	12–3 am							
4th Watch	3–6 am							
5th Watch	6–9 am							
6th Watch	9–12 pm							
7th Watch	12–3 pm							
8th Watch	3–6 pm							

"The world does not need a definition of religion as much as it needs a demonstration."
Martin Luther

Weekly Plan Synopsis *(See Appendix for full plan)*

Day 1
Telling yourself and God the truth about where you are in your heart today! Repent and commit it to God.

Day 2
Pray Psalms 51 in the first person tense for yourself, no matter who has hurt or betrayed you.

Day 3
Continue as an action of intent to forgive. Forgiveness is not a feeling -- but a commandment (to do). Release yourself from the torment, you deserve it. Pray "By faith (trust in God's ability) I choose to forgive those who have caused me pain in Jesus Name. I forgive name them as an act of faith.

Day 4
Begin thanking God for restoring your peace and for his forgiveness because you held onto unforgiveness in your heart!

Day 5
Wherefore my dearly beloved, flee from idolatry. (I Corinthians 10:13-14) Anything that occupies the space in our heart that belongs to God is idolatry.

Day 6
Could you be the one to share the gospel with them and save them from a burning hell! Remember one plants, another waters, and God gives the increase!

Day 7
What fruit can you pick from the Tree of Life to feed your heart today get started feeding the scriptures to your heart to manifest that fruit.

Week Fifty: Covetous Heart
Reference: Weekly Plan Outline (See Appendix)

Every day tell yourself the truth, face that truth no matter how ugly it is, repent of it and commit it to God. This is an action not a feeling; you do it by faith continuously until you feel the release in your spirit or until it is no longer a chore but a pleasure!

What is a Covetous Heart?

Hebrew: batsa`

Greek: pleonexia

Remember Jesus has proven himself faithful so that engrafted and adopted sons would receive the anointing to be faithful through his obedience to the Father.

Psalms 10:3-8 For the wicked boasteth of his heart's desire, and blesseth the covetous, *whom* the LORD abhorreth. ⁴ The wicked, through the pride of his countenance, will not seek *after God*: God *is* not in all his thoughts. ⁵ His ways are always grievous; thy judgments *are* far above out of his sight: *as for* all his enemies, he puffeth at them. ⁶ He hath said in his heart, I shall not be moved: for *I shall* never *be* in adversity. ⁷ His mouth is full of cursing and deceit and fraud: under his tongue *is* mischief and vanity. ⁸ He sitteth in the lurking places of the villages: in the secret places doth he murder the innocent: his eyes are privily set against the poor.

Week Fifty: Covetous Heart

Take comfort in the following passage(s):

Luke 8:4-21 And when much people were gathered together, and were come to him out of every city, he spake by a parable: ⁵ A sower went out to sow his seed: and as he sowed, some fell by the way side; and it was trodden down, and the fowls of the air devoured it. ¹¹ Now the parable is this: The seed is the word of God. ¹² Those by the way side are they that hear; then cometh the devil, and taketh away the word out of their hearts, lest they should believe and be saved. ¹³ They on the rock *are they*, which, when they hear, receive the word with joy; and these have no root, which for a while believe, and in time of temptation fall away. ¹⁴ And that which fell among thorns are they, which, when they have heard, go forth, and are choked with cares and riches and pleasures of *this* life, and bring no fruit to perfection. ¹⁵ But that on the good ground are they, which in an honest and good heart, having heard the word, keep *it*, and bring forth fruit with patience.

What Weights and Burdens Come to Mind to Lay Down?

_____

_____

YOUR PERSONAL COMMITMENT TO GOD

Thanksgiving – Praise – Worship Your Way into His Presence
Opening Prayer (Remember Put on Your Armour!)
Scripture(s) Reading

Call to Action for the Day
Will I chose to believe the truth I've discovered?
Will I allow the truth to change my thinking and my conduct?
We must adjust ourselves to the Bible— never the Bible to ourselves.
Closing Prayer

Week Fifty: Covetous Heart

GODS COMMITMENT TO YOU

Promises from the Father _____

_____

Priorities of the Day_____

_____

Benefits for the Day_____

_____

DECLARATIONS AND DECREES

Protection_____

_____

Strategies for the Day_____

_____

Week Fifty: Covetous Heart
PRAISE REPORT

Cool of the Day Revelation_____

WEEK Fifty One

CALENDAR

Day		Sat	Sun	Mon	Tue	Wed	Thu	Fri
Date	Hour							
1st Watch	6–9 pm							
2nd Watch	9–12 am							
3rd Watch	12–3 am							
4th Watch	3–6 am							
5th Watch	6–9 am							
6th Watch	9–12 pm							
7th Watch	12–3 pm							
8th Watch	3–6 pm							

"One of the pastors startled the group with the declaration that "My grandmother's translation is the best I've ever read." To which his colleagues exclaimed "What! Your grandmother translated the Bible?" To which he responded "Yes, she translated the Bible into her life, and was the most powerful translation I've ever seen!" Needless to say, the group of pastors got the point!"
Unknown

Weekly Plan Synopsis *(See Appendix for full plan)*

Day 1
Telling yourself and God the truth about where you are in your heart today! Repent and commit it to God.

Day 2
Pray Psalms 51 in the first person tense for yourself, no matter who has hurt or betrayed you.

Day 3
Continue as an action of intent to forgive. Forgiveness is not a feeling -- but a commandment (to do). Release yourself from the torment, you deserve it. Pray "By faith (trust in God's ability) I choose to forgive those who have caused me pain in Jesus Name. I forgive name them as an act of faith.

Day 4
Begin thanking God for restoring your peace and for his forgiveness because you held onto unforgiveness in your heart!

Day 5
Wherefore my dearly beloved, flee from idolatry. (I Corinthians 10:13-14) Anything that occupies the space in our heart that belongs to God is idolatry.

Day 6
Could you be the one to share the gospel with them and save them from a burning hell! Remember one plants, another waters, and God gives the increase!

Day 7
What fruit can you pick from the Tree of Life to feed your heart today get started feeding the scriptures to your heart to manifest that fruit.

Week Fifty-One: Whole Heart
Reference: Weekly Plan Outline (See Appendix)

Every day tell yourself the truth, face that truth no matter how ugly it is, repent of it and commit it to God. This is an action not a feeling; you do it by faith continuously until you feel the release in your spirit or until it is no longer a chore but a pleasure!

What is a Whole Heart?
inner man, mind, will, heart, understanding, conscience, heart (of moral character), as seat of appetites, as seat of emotions and passions, as seat of courage

Hebrew: leb
Greek: sozo

Remember Jesus has proven himself faithful so that engrafted and adopted sons would receive the anointing to be faithful through his obedience to the Father.

Psalms 138:1-8 ¹ I will praise thee with my whole heart: before the gods will I sing praise unto thee. ² I will worship toward thy holy temple, and praise thy name for thy lovingkindness and for thy truth: for thou hast magnified thy word above all thy name. ³ In the day when I cried thou answeredst me, *and* strengthenedst me *with* strength in my soul. ⁴ All the kings of the earth shall praise thee, O LORD, when they hear the words of thy mouth. ⁵ Yea, they shall sing in the ways of the LORD: for great *is* the glory of the LORD.   ⁶ Though the LORD *be* high, yet hath he respect unto the lowly: but the proud he knoweth afar off. ⁷ Though I walk in the midst of trouble, thou wilt revive me: thou shalt stretch forth thine hand against the wrath of mine enemies, and thy right hand shall save me. ⁸ The LORD will perfect *that which* concerneth me: thy mercy, O LORD, *endureth* for ever: forsake not the works of thine own hands.

Week Fifty-One: Whole Heart

Take comfort in the following passage(s):
Jude 1:1-7 **1** Jude, the servant of Jesus Christ, and brother of James, to them that are sanctified by God the Father, and preserved in Jesus Christ, *and* called: **2** Mercy unto you, and peace, and love, be multiplied. **3** Beloved, when I gave all diligence to write unto you of the common salvation, it was needful for me to write unto you, and exhort *you* that ye should earnestly contend for the faith which was once delivered unto the saints. **4** For there are certain men crept in unawares, who were before of old ordained to this condemnation, ungodly men, turning the grace of our God into lasciviousness, and denying the only Lord God, and our Lord Jesus Christ. **5** I will therefore put you in remembrance, though ye once knew this, how that the Lord, having saved the people out of the land of Egypt, afterward destroyed them that believed not. **6** And the angels which kept not their first estate, but left their own habitation, he hath reserved in everlasting chains under darkness unto the judgment of the great day. **7** Even as Sodom and Gomorrha, and the cities about them in like manner, giving themselves over to fornication, and going after strange flesh, are set forth for an example, suffering the vengeance of eternal fire.

What Weights and Burdens Come to Mind to Lay Down?

_____

_____

YOUR PERSONAL COMMITMENT TO GOD
Thanksgiving – Praise – Worship Your Way into His Presence
Opening Prayer (Remember Put on Your Armour!)
Scripture(s) Reading
Call to Action for the Day
Will I chose to believe the truth I've discovered?
Will I allow the truth to change my thinking and my conduct?
We must adjust ourselves to the Bible— never the Bible to ourselves.
Closing Prayer

Week Fifty-One: Whole Heart

GODS COMMITMENT TO YOU

Promises from the Father _____

_____

Priorities of the Day_____

_____

Benefits for the Day_____

_____

DECLARATIONS AND DECREES

Protection_____

_____

Strategies for the Day_____

_____

Week Fifty-One: Whole Heart

PRAISE REPORT

Cool of the Day Revelation_____

WEEK Fifty Two

CALENDAR

Day		Sat	Sun	Mon	Tue	Wed	Thu	Fri
Date	Hour							
1st Watch	6–9 pm							
2nd Watch	9–12 am							
3rd Watch	12–3 am							
4th Watch	3–6 am							
5th Watch	6–9 am							
6th Watch	9–12 pm							
7th Watch	12–3 pm							
8th Watch	3–6 pm							

"Lay hold on the Bible until the Bible lays hold on you"
Will H. Houghton

Weekly Plan Synopsis *(See Appendix for full plan)*

Day 1
Telling yourself and God the truth about where you are in your heart today! Repent and commit it to God.

Day 2
Pray Psalms 51 in the first person tense for yourself, no matter who has hurt or betrayed you.

Day 3
Continue as an action of intent to forgive. Forgiveness is not a feeling -- but a commandment (to do). Release yourself from the torment, you deserve it. Pray "By faith (trust in God's ability) I choose to forgive those who have caused me pain in Jesus Name. I forgive name them as an act of faith.

Day 4
Begin thanking God for restoring your peace and for his forgiveness because you held onto unforgiveness in your heart!

Day 5
Wherefore my dearly beloved, flee from idolatry. (I Corinthians 10:13-14) Anything that occupies the space in our heart that belongs to God is idolatry.

Day 6
Could you be the one to share the gospel with them and save them from a burning hell! Remember one plants, another waters, and God gives the increase!

Day 7
What fruit can you pick from the Tree of Life to feed your heart today get started feeding the scriptures to your heart to manifest that fruit.

Week Fifty-Two: Whole Heart (II)
Reference: Weekly Plan Outline (See Appendix)

Every day tell yourself the truth, face that truth no matter how ugly it is, repent of it and commit it to God. This is an action not a feeling; you do it by faith continuously until you feel the release in your spirit or until it is no longer a chore but a pleasure!

What is a Whole Heart II?
inner man, mind, will, heart, soul, understanding, mind, knowledge, thinking, reflection, memory, inclination, resolution, determination (of will)as seat of emotions and passions, as seat of courage and that which breathes, the breathing substance or being, soul, the inner being of man, living being (with life in the blood), the man himself, self, person or individual, activity of mind, activity of the will, activity of the character

Hebrew: lebab
Greek: nephesh

Remember Jesus has proven himself faithful so that engrafted and adopted sons would receive the anointing to be faithful through his obedience to the Father.

Psalms 119:58 I intreated thy favour with my whole heart: be merciful unto me according to thy word. 59 I thought on my ways, and turned my feet unto thy testimonies. 60 I made haste, and delayed not to keep thy commandments. 61 The bands of the wicked have robbed me: but I have not forgotten thy law. 62 At midnight I will rise to give thanks unto thee because of thy righteous judgments. 63 I am a companion of all them that fear thee, and of them that keep thy precepts. 64 The earth, O LORD, is full of thy mercy: teach me thy statutes.

Week Fifty-Two: Whole Heart II

Take comfort in the following passage(s):
Psalms 119:"... 85 The proud have digged pits for me, which are not after thy law. 86 All thy commandments are faithful: they persecute me wrongfully; help thou me. 87 They had almost consumed me upon earth; but I forsook not thy precepts. 88 Quicken me after thy lovingkindness; so shall I keep the testimony of thy mouth. 89 For ever, O LORD, thy word is settled in heaven. 90 Thy faithfulness is unto all generations:...101 I have refrained my feet from every evil way, that I might keep thy word... 111 Thy testimonies have I taken as an heritage for ever: for they are the rejoicing of my heart. 112 I have inclined mine heart to perform thy statutes alway, even unto the end....116 Uphold me according unto thy word, that I may live: and let me not be ashamed of my hope. 117 Hold thou me up, and I shall be safe: and I will have respect unto thy statutes continually....127 Therefore I love thy commandments above gold; yea, above fine gold...133 Order my steps in thy word:...145 I cried with my whole heart; hear me, O LORD: I will keep thy statutes. 146 I cried unto thee; save me, and I shall keep thy testimonies."

What Weights and Burdens Come to Mind to Lay Down?

_____

_____

YOUR PERSONAL COMMITMENT TO GOD
Thanksgiving – Praise – Worship Your Way into His Presence
Opening Prayer (Remember Put on Your Armour!)
Scripture(s) Reading
Call to Action for the Day
Will I chose to believe the truth I've discovered?
Will I allow the truth to change my thinking and my conduct?
We must adjust ourselves to the Bible— never the Bible to ourselves.
Closing Prayer

Week Fifty-Two: Whole Heart II

GODS COMMITMENT TO YOU

Promises from the Father _____

_____

Priorities of the Day_____

_____

Benefits for the Day_____

_____

DECLARATIONS AND DECREES

Protection_____

_____

Strategies for the Day_____

_____

Week Fifty-Two: Whole Heart II

PRAISE REPORT

Cool of the Day Revelation_____

The Lord they God, he it is that doth go with thee; he will not fail thee nor forsake thee. Deuteronomy 31:6

Personal Notes:

The Lord they God, he it is that doth go with thee; he will not fail thee nor forsake thee. Deuteronomy 31:6

Personal Notes:

The Lord they God, he it is that doth go with thee; he will not fail thee nor forsake thee. Deuteronomy 31:6

Personal Notes:

The Lord they God, he it is that doth go with thee; he will not fail thee nor forsake thee. Deuteronomy 31:6

Personal Notes:

APPENDIX

It would have been wonderful to place this within the body of every week but due to a sizeable change in the volumes pages this was not considered the best approach.

For your convenience should you choose to copy these pages in this Appendix or gingerly cut them from this location for ease of reference; permission is granted!

Be Blessed!

Patricia E Adams

Significance of Day and Time of Devotion

Which Day of the Week to Begin?

Suggestion:

Begin your week on Saturday and follow the Jewish Calendar as oppose to the Gregorian Calendar which we commonly use. Why? There is a blessing in being in step with Gods' timing – it is not about a race of people, but the timing of God. This suggestion is to step into the flow of an anointing that rested on the tribe of Isacchar! It is merely a suggestion, proceed as you desire.

What Time of Day to Begin?

Jesus had a way of saying early in the morning will I seek his face. The day in spiritual terms are divided into 8 watches of 3 hours each. From Sunset to Sunrise, in general 6 p.m. to 6 p.m. the following day.

```
6 p.m. – 9 p.m.           First Watch
9 p.m. – 12 a.m.  Second Watch
12 a.m. – 3 a.m.  Third Watch
3 a.m. – 6 a.m.           Fourth Watch
6 a.m. – 9 a.m.           Fifth Watch
9 a.m. – 12 p.m.  Sixth Watch
12 p.m. – 3 p.m.  Seventh Watch
3 p.m. – 6 p.m.           Eighth Watch
```

What Is the Significance of the Time of Day?

Each 3 hour period is called a watch. The First to the Second Watches order your day. The Third to the Fifth Watches REINFORCES the prayer hedges that have been established in the First to Second Watches. The Sixth to the Eighth Watch is being alert and sober awaiting instructions and quenching fiery darts (it is the little foxes that spoil the vine). Get rid of the little foxes that ruin the vineyards as Solomon said in Song of Songs 2:15

The Danger of Little Things

Excerpt from Bob Gass "On Colorado's long peak, lies the remains of a giant 400-year-old tree. Age, storms, and avalanches, couldn't bring it down. What did? A tiny beetle you could crush under your foot. It ate right through the bark and devoured its heart.

Be careful, it's the little foxes that ruin the vineyards. Little attitudes; but if you practice them often enough, they become fixed attitudes. Little indulgences; but if you give place to them long enough, they desensitize you to sin. Remember when certain things bothered you? Now you don't give them a second thought. You're being desensitized!

Every alcoholic started by telling himself, "I can handle it." Every victim of Internet pornography (and they're getting younger every day), started with a look, got hooked on a fantasy, and ended up uncaging a tiger that:
(a) can devour them; (b) will never willingly go back into its cage.

Before a moral problem got out of hand in the Corinthian church, Paul hit it head on. Listen, "I also received a report...One of your men is sleeping with his step-mother. And you're so above it all that it doesn't even faze you. You pass it off as a small thing, but it's anything but that. Yeast, too, is a 'small thing,' but it works its way through a whole batch...get rid of this 'yeast'" (1Corinthians 5:1-7 TM). Strong language!

Why does God make such a big deal out of this anyway? Because sin hurts us, and anything that hurts one of His children, makes Him angry." You are interacting with others during the Sixth to the Eighth watch that are predominantly outside of your inner circle during the course of a business day. You have prepared yourself to have listening ears, heart and spirit attuned to the voice of God, so when God says move you move, and when God says stop you stop, in other words you are training yourself to walk with God like Enoch and how God intended for us to walk when he created Adam. To meet with him, walk with him in the cool of the day! Walk In the Spirit!

How Do We Walk in the Spirit – Surrendered

Surrender means to yield ownership, to relinquish control over what we consider ours: our property, our time, our "rights."

Stewards over what belongs to someone else – God!

Giving God total control of every jot and tittles of our lives!

It is the Greatest Decision and the Best Decision you will ever make in your life! Your chooser and picker have been broken from birth, and to acknowledge that if we had wanted what he wanted from the beginning our lives would be flawlessly fulfilled! Let Go of Your Way and Take the Assignment of doing it His Way!

Why?

He Loves US and wants what is best for us – our brains weigh science says all of about 3 pounds! How can a finite measurable piece of matter tell the one who measured that matter how their lives should go! How can the clay say to the potter make me this way! Yet He gives us a free will to choose to do it our way, and he will never take that from us! Like the movie star said that he would not let go until they pried it from his cold dead hands, God will let you have it your way like that too!

What are you holding onto like that?

It is your right to do it your way and your freedom of choice? Your right to the pursuit of happiness that the government says you can have? Or some mess you created and called it your world? Are you really happy with the choice you have made so far?

Well if you said no, then let's go about the business of exchanging wills through the way of escape Jesus has made for us as surrendered his right to stay in Heaven and to never die for your sins and mine!

He surrendered more than we will ever surrender! Clearly, he said if we will save our lives we will lose them, but if we will surrender our lives we would gain life! So why not try it this way, His way!

In John 3 Christ choice to surrender His right to be God, again in Matthew 4 and finally He surrendered His right to live for himself! Because he died and rose again and is alive forever more we simply have to give up our way and accept him as our Lord and Savior and believe and have faith in Him and obey the Word of God.

Paul said he died daily to do the will of God and we are no different! To live as He deems for us to live will require a daily decision to wake up and surrender control of your life and choose to walk it out as he has planned!

We are saved, so we have Him as our Savior! Since we have accepted the gift of salvation, have you made him Lord (owner) of your life?

This is where surrender steps in and says I am not my own, but I have been bought with a price and it is my good pleasure to do my masters bidding! Mary Magdalene had the idea when she clinged to Jesus and fell at his feet with gratitude for getting her out of her broken mess she had made from her own decisions!

Jeremiah 29:11 says that God has a plan and a purpose! Don't you want to know what it is?

He will order your steps aright when you determine you want to live your life in his plan and not your own! It will not be comfortable, like breaking in a new pair of shoes it will hurt for a while, but then the shoe surrenders to the shape of your foot or you have to get rid of them or live in pain! Personally, find it difficult to break in new shoes, I look for shoes that are formed the way my foot is formed and spend less time in pain because I am only getting use to the fabric and not the form of the shoe. God has a form for your life and the fabric he wants to adorn you in!

He has the blueprint for your life and the material to build it! His vision sees further down the process than your vision can see "where there is no vision," the people will perish. Where there is limited vision there is obstructions ahead, my paraphrase!

You have one opportunity to get it done! Then after that opportunity comes the judgment! What percentage of Gods plan and purpose for your life will you get accomplished or leave undone and plant in the cemetery! The cemetery is a wealthy place! So many gifted and talented people who died full and not emptied or imparted into the plan of God in the universe!

The calling of God and the gifts are God are without repentance. Let's look at how his word bares out that He is intentional and congruent with his desires for us! His words and his actions line up, that says He wants us to have great success if we would seek him for his way he will not suffer our foot to be moved!

- "Where there is no vision, the people perish." (Proverbs 29:18)

- "For I know the thoughts that I think toward you, says the Lord, thoughts of peace and not of evil, **to give you a future** and a hope." (Jeremiah 29:11)

- "Your eyes saw my substance, being yet unformed. And in Your book they all were written, the days **fashioned** for me, when as yet there were none of them." (Psalm 139:16)

- "Since his days are **determined**, the number of his months is with You; You have appointed his limits, so that he cannot pass." (Job 14:5)

- "And we know that all things work together for good to those who love God, to those who are called **according to His purpose**." (Romans 8:28)

- "For many are called, but few are chosen." (Matthew 22:14)

Determined and fashioned" plans for as long as the earth remaineth, and seedtime and harvest! Heaven and Earth will pass away, but his Word will be forever! You and I will pass away, but His Word, His Will for his creation will never change! What a plan!

Do you still want to sing "I Did It My Way"?

The blind leading the blind - when He promises to give us sight that exceeds natural abilities by being a lamp unto our feet and a light unto our pathway! He will order your steps on every hand; from marriage, careers and ministry! We have compassed this same mountain long enough don't you think? It is time to go up and possess the land!

Caleb and Joshua said they were well able to go up when God first told them that the land was theirs, but because they were surrounded by wavering and self-willed people they had to wait for them to vanquish in the way they chose over the way God had chosen for them!

When they did go up to possess the land they got the directions right and got there and discovered that the people the others had thought would see them as grasshoppers, had been living in fear of them all of those years because they had heard how God had brought them out of the land of Egypt!

They had expected them 40 years sooner to come in and depose them from the land! How long will we stand halted between two opinions? If God is God then serve Him!

The Bible says that unless God builds the "house" we will labor in vain trying to do it all on our own. Foundations are laid by God that we see in Isaiah where he made highways in the wilderness so that the animals would not devour them! How does this happen? When our wills are surrendered to the point where God can create and birth in us his divine plan!

- "For as many are led by the Spirit of God, these are the sons of God." (Romans 8:14)
- "The steps of a good man are ordered by the Lord ..." (Psalm 37:23)
- "O Lord, I know the way of a man is not in himself; it is not in man who walks to direct his own steps." (Jeremiah 10:23)
- "There is a way which seems right to a man, but its end is the way of death." (Proverbs 14:12)
- "A man's steps are of the Lord. How then can a man understand his own way?" (Proverbs 20:24)
- "A man's heart plans his way, but the Lord directs his steps." (Proverbs 16:9)
- "Direct my steps by Your word, and let no iniquity have dominion over me." (Psalm 119:133)
- "Therefore be followers of God as dear children." (Ephesians 5:1)
- "My sheep hear My voice, and I know them, and they follow Me." (John 10:27)
- "Trust in the Lord with all your heart, and lean not on your own understanding; in all your ways acknowledge Him, and He shall direct your paths." (Proverbs 3:5)
- "The Lord is my Shepherd; I shall not want. He makes me to lie down in green pastures; He leads me beside the still waters. He restores my soul; He leads me in the paths of righteousness for His name's sake." (Psalm 23:1)
- Thus says the Lord, your Redeemer, the Holy One of Israel: "I am the Lord your God, who teaches you to profit, who leads you by the way you should go." (Isaiah 48:17)
- "Show me Your ways, O Lord; teach me Your paths. Lead me in Your truth and teach me, for You are the God of my salvation ..." (Psalm 25:4)
- "I will instruct you and teach you in the way you should go; I will guide you with My eye." (Psalm 32:8)
- "Teach me Your way, O Lord, and lead me in a smooth path, because of my enemies." (Psalm 27:11)
- "The Lord will guide you continually ..." (Isaiah 58:11)

- "For this is God, our God forever and ever; He will be our guide even to death." (Psalm 48:14)
- "Moreover You led them by day with a cloudy pillar, and by night with a pillar of fire, to give them light on the road which they should travel." (Nehemiah 9:12)
- "All we like sheep have gone astray; we have turned, every one, to his own way ..." (Isaiah 53:6)
- "Therefore you shall be careful to do as the Lord Your God has commanded you; You shall not turn aside to the right hand or to the left." (Deuteronomy 5:32)

We become Sons of God when we are:

- Led by the Spirit of God
- The steps of a good man are ordered by the Lord
- It is not in man who walks to direct his own steps
- A way which seems right to a man ... its end is the way of death
- A man's steps are of the Lord
- The Lord directs his steps
- Direct my steps by Your Word
- Be followers of God as dear children
- My sheep hear My voice ... and they follow Me
- He shall direct your paths
- He leads me by still waters
- He leads me in the paths of righteousness
- Leads you by the way you should go
- Lead me in your truth
- I will guide you with My eye
- Lead me in a smooth path
- The Lord will guide you continually
- He will be our guide even to death
- Led them by day ... to give them light on the road which they should travel

"Neither Wast Thou Washed...[Nor] Salted...Nor Swaddled."
Ezekiel 16:4

(1) You must be washed by "the washing of water by the Word" (Eph 5:26)

(2) You must be salted as a newborn baby was in Jewish tradition rubbed with salt to toughen their skins and to prevent bruising – reducing the need for "special handling."

(3) You must be swaddled - covered and protected through fellowship that holds you accountable to remain committed to God.

A few names of some who suffered dire consequences for not surrendering totally to follow God:

Adam, Eve, Cain, Moses, Jacob and David

Why have we as Christians not entered into our Promised Land on Earth! I find no fault in God, but in us as Christians! It is a place to be entered into by following the directions completely!

First –

We must Pray!

Father,

In the name of Jesus, I fully surrender physically, spiritually and emotionally to your will for my life! Give me directions for your divine will for my life and order my steps in Your Word! Sanctify me from the roots of my tree and lead me beside still waters and restore my soul, and lead me in a plain path! I thank you and praise you for all that you have done, are doing and going to do in my life in Jesus Name, Amen!

Secondly –

We must Pray that we will remain!

Father,

In the name of Jesus, I have surrendered my whole self to you from now until eternity and I believe that you will not allow me to go astray, but lead me in the plain path of righteousness that you have designed and fashioned for me from the time you had me on your mind! I thank you and praise you for keeping me, because I desire to be kept! In Jesus Name, Amen!

What does God think about your choice?

- "Unless the Lord builds the house, they labor in vain who build it." (Psalm 127:1)

What does God say about being Lord of your life?

- "Therefore whoever hears these sayings of Mine, and does them, I will liken him to a wise man who built his house on the rock; and the rain descended, the floods came, and the winds blew and beat on that house; and it did not fall, for it was founded on the rock. Now everyone who hears these sayings of Mine, and does not do them, will be like a foolish man who built his house on the sand: and the rain descended, the floods came, and the winds blew and beat on that house, and it fell. And great was its fall." (Matthew 7:24)

How Does God Reward Your Choice?

- "... I have set before you life and death, blessing and cursing; therefore choose life, that both you and your descendants may live, that you may love the Lord your God, that you may obey His voice, and that you may cling to Him, for He is your life and the length of your days ..." (Deuteronomy 30:19)

Naturally you will try to get back on the throne of your life, and perhaps you will! But you now know the way down off the throne! I Beseech YOU by the Mercies of God through Christ Jesus that you run the race that is before you and not turn around and lose ground – in the name of Jesus! AMEN!

Why? Paul is about to tell you –

- "For though I am free from all men, I have made myself a servant to all, that I might win the more." (1 Corinthians 9:19)

You were bought at a price; do not become slaves of men. Brethren, let each one remain with God in that calling in which he was called." (1 Corinthians 7:23)

How will you know you are progressing?

- You shall know a tree by the fruit it bears!

There are 9 Parts to the Fruit of the Spirit:

Galatians 5:22 "But the fruit of the Spirit, is love, joy, peace, longsuffering, gentleness, goodness, faith, meekness, temperance, against such there is no law."

There Are 17 Works Of The Flesh:

So Galatians 5:1 says, "Stand fast therefore in the liberty, wherewith Christ hath made us free, and be not entangled again with the yoke of bondage. In this case unforgiveness! Galatians 5:16, says "Walk (follow) in the spirit, and ye shall not fulfill the lust of the flesh.

How do you walk in the spirit? Someone asked how do you eat an elephant, and the response was "One bite at a time." So take a bite of the fruit of the spirit one bite at a time until you have eaten the whole fruit! If not, you will work harder in Satan's camp than you ever will in God's! Now let's follow Christ day-by-day!

Weekly Plan Outline: Day 1

Saturday Remember Put on Your Armour!

Begin the Week by telling yourself and God the truth about where you are in your heart today! Then face that truth no matter how ugly it is. Repent and commit it to God. Why tell God the truth – doesn't he already know – you are wondering? Yes he does know, but this is about you and with the mouth confession is made unto salvation! Confession is with the intent to become transparent and removing the cloak of shame from your heart!

DAILY
Put on the Whole Armour as a Lifestyle!

Helmet of Salvation
to keep my thoughts aligned with your will

Loins Girt with Truth
to keep me in integrity

Breastplate of Righteousness protect my standing in the community

Gospel of Peace
to order my steps correctly

Shield of Faith
to secure my purpose and destiny

Sword of the Spirit
to reign, rule and have dominion

Weekly Plan Outline: Day 2

Sunday Remember Put on Your Armour!

Pray Psalms 51 in the first person tense for yourself, no matter who has hurt or betrayed you. What role did you play in what happened to you, perhaps you were an innocent child, or a willing participant until things went sour -- what happened to cause your heart to be broken. Admit blame if there is any, because if you had a choice to stay in a bad relationship or go, and you chose to stay -- take responsibility for that part. If you were an innocent child or youth, how has what happened to you affected your today -- are you still a victim of the predator. Today you can choose by faith to no longer be the victim -- one day, one minute, one second at a time until you are completely free in Jesus Name! This is a universal truth, 'For every cause there is a reaction.' We are responsible for the decisions we make and the relationships we entertain. Perhaps you were violated physically, emotionally , sexually and socially -- all without cause, but God has made a way of escape for you from all of these violations! Forgive! He doesn't want you walking around with the aftermath of the wars that have been waged against you as a badge of honor. Whatever it was -- you are still here, and God is still able!

Psalms 119:165 says we are to take no offense. When we take offense we take that person who offended us and tie them to our bodies and carry them around as weights. Weights that prevent us from entering into the doors of blessings God has prepared for us. Unlatch the bodies so you can enter into the rest of God for your soul, and be healed in the name of the Lord!

Weekly Plan Outline: Day 3

Monday Remember Put on Your Armour!

Continue as an action of intent to forgive. Forgiveness is not a feeling -- but a commandment (to do). Release yourself from the torment, you deserve it. Pray "By faith (trust in God's ability) I choose to forgive those who have caused me pain in Jesus Name. I forgive name them as an act of faith. You may be feeling anger, rage, teeth grinding and fist clenching emotions rise up inside. So, in the name of Jesus I speak peace to your spirit, soul, mind and body. I bind you Satan from the heart of this one. I command you to release this one now in the name of Jesus! Amen! Father give your angels charge over them to preserve them during this time of pain! Now! Thank God for peace, joy, grace, and forgiveness. Ask him to wash you and purge you with hyssop. Confess this scripture. "Behold, thou desirest truth in the inward parts: and in the hidden part thou shalt make me to know wisdom. Make me to hear joy and gladness: that the bones which thou has broken may rejoice. Hide thy face from my sins, and blot out all mine iniquities, Create in a me a clean heart, O God, and renew a right spirit within me. Cast me not away from thy presence; and take not thy holy spirit from me. Restore unto me the joy of thy salvation; and uphold me with thy free spirit." (Psalms 51:6-12)

Weekly Plan Outline: Day 4

Tuesday Remember Put on Your Armour!

Begin thanking God for restoring your peace and his forgiveness because you held onto unforgiveness in your heart. Satan knows we must forgive so he impedes us with a belief we have a right to unforgiveness! To obtain the blessings He desires to bestow on us we must be broken. Brokenness in its' purest form is to desire to walk in God's perfect will for your life. The safest place in the world is in the arms of Jesus, a songwriter penned! How we handle what has happened to us and who did things to us will determine how the anointing will be able to flow through us! Unforgiveness causes spiritual blockage! God's grace is sufficient in all times, all seasons of your life as a vessel that has been damaged by the warfare of life waged against, comes traumas aftermath; shame, humiliation and other collateral damages. Despair not! Remember "What shall we say to these things? (rape, murder, persecution, rejections on every hand, etc.) If God be for us…. Then what shall separate us from the love of Christ? …tribulation, distress, persecution, famine, nakedness, peril, nor sword?...I am persuaded, that neither death, life, angels, principalities, powers, things present, things to come, height, depth, nor creature, shall separate us from the love of God, which is in Christ Jesus our Lord. (Romans 8:31-39)

Weekly Plan Outline: Day 5

Wednesday Remember Put on Your Armour!

But God has made a way of escape through his son Jesus Christ! "There hath no temptation taken you but such as is common to man; but God is faithful, who will not suffer you to be tempted above that ye are able, but with the temptation also make a way of escape, that ye may be able to bear it. Wherefore my dearly beloved, flee from idolatry. (I Corinthians 10:13-14) Anything that occupies the space in our heart the belongs to God is idolatry. The issues of the past that we nurse, are a form of idolatry -- and the pain has become our God. We feed the pain medications, alcohol and illicit relationships in an effort to appease the beast! But remember not to be entangled again with the yoke of bondage. Every time you feel that pain returning, or resurfacing as you see the person or persons who caused you pain -- remember to forgive by faith until it becomes manifested. That is faith, it is the evidence of things hoped for and the evidence of things not seen. You reach for it, grab hold of it and hold onto it until it manifest itself as yours. At this point I want you to see that the person and the spirit behind the person who hurt you are two separate issues. Under the control of Satan the person(s) or persons did to you what they would not have done to themselves. Can't you see how Satan is the originator of abuse. He promises people fame and fortune, uses them and discards them when he is finished destroying them. He is a father who abuses his own children. Allow God to pour out your heart in mercy to the one who mistreated you, and pray for God to send laborers in their path to release them from the snare of Satan. God does not expect you to embrace your perpetrator in any form. What he does require is obedience to His will! I say this because there are those who have harmed me that God asked me if I would write a letter to them expressing what affect their crime had on my life, and then to go so far as to personally stand before them and confront them with the crime! God deals with us individually as he knows us better than we know ourselves! I am not recommending you do the same, because without God's leading you may find yourself in harms way! If there is no peace in the instructions you are about to embark on – then do not pursue! David inquired of God "shall I pursue" and God said "Yes" in addition to Yes he said he would give them into his hands to overtake! When God says pursue that is when you pursue! OTHERWISE STAND DOWN! Because God will right every wrong! It is yours to forgive and Gods' to revenge!

    When Jesus died on the Cross of Calvary and uttered with his lips to His Father to forgive his perpetrators – he made provision for an anointing if you would a gift of forgiveness to be accessible to every believer when faced with such crisis. It is up to us to access that anointing, because he will not force it on you! God gives us the grace to forgive through the final breath that was on Jesus' lips while on the cross. "Father forgive, them for they know not what they do." Through all the things that Satan meant for evil to destroy you, God has turned and is turning them around for your good. Since, you are reading this book it is evident that the hardship did not destroy you! Maybe it did someone else you know, but GODhas a plan! In Jeremiah 29:11 He says "For I know the thoughts that I think towards you, saith the Lord, thoughts of peace, and not of evil, to give you an expected end." Evil lies in the heart of men and they choose to hurt by free will, yielding their members as instruments of evil. But because God who at all times kept you on every hand from losing your mind. You are still here to turn around and bruise the head of Satan for what he has done to you and your family. I am still here to tell you that God is a restoring God and that He will repay the evil that has been done to you. The people who allowed Satan to use them, are of all people most miserable. May not look like it on the outside, but on the inside it is an ugly state of being. They have to not only bear the mark of what they did, but they have to face God's judgment! Pray to the Lord of the Harvest to send someone to lead them home! Because we are to pray for our enemies! Not because we want to see them go free of any penalties, that is not your place! God said the wages of sin are death, there is spiritual death that exist among the living! Some of your perpertrators called themselves Christians, and I say called themselves! Gods' Word clearly tells us that many call on his name but their hearts are far from him! Being the Judge and Jury sentences you to a state of deadness! It is difficult for you to get the full measure of living out of your life, because death is laying in the midst of your heart!

Weekly Plan Outline: Day 6

Thursday Remember Put on Your Armour!

Could you be the one to share the gospel with them and save them from a burning hell. If that seems farfetched to you, I understand, but I promise you it can happen, and has happened! Remember one plants, another waters, and God gives the increase! Again this is not an expectation from God in the natural! To accomplish this God would have to place an anointing on you that would empower you to witness to someone who has injured you without malice in your heart! Only Pursue When GOD says Pursue!

You don't have to get up close and personal. God knows the wound is fresh. You could opt to send what I will call a 'Salvation Letter' and tell the individual(s) how you feel and let them know that God has been faithful to relieve you of the weight of what was done to you by them without a return address. And that you would like to extend that same offer to them. Tell them you forgave them by faith, and that God will forgiven them, and help them to forgive themselves too. Tell them you love them through Christ Jesus. God teaches us how to love the unlovely, because we too were once unlovely and guilty of death.

Weekly Plan Outline: Day 7

Friday Remember Put on Your Armour!

The number of Perfection. " Being confident of this very thing that, He who hath begun a good work in you (is able to) will perform it until the day of Jesus Christ." (Philippians 1:6) Today is fruit picking day. What fruit can you pick from the Tree of Life to feed your heart today. Choose one or two and get started eating the scriptures that apply to that particular fruit. You have emptied out the works of the flesh from your heart, and that requires that you put something in its place to prevent the crop from returning 7 fold. This number we call perfection comes forth as we are shaken to the very core of our being! During years with the number 7 on them I have found myself personally in a season of conflicting moments! It is like a Charles Dickens – Tale of Two Cities (It was the best of times and the worst of times) all at the same time! How could you be in such crisis on one hand, have a thunderstorm on one side of your life and the Sun shining on the other side! Well it is called life, but it is also a time that comes when God needs to see if He can trust you with His Blessings! Will you turn back at the least bit of distressing moments, or will you set your face like flint and declare that as for me and my house we will serve the Lord! I will not look back like Lots wife, and I will not be denied like Moses' at the mouth of the manifestation of the promises of God in my life! Whatever has happened to you up to now – God says is no comparison to what he has in store for those who love him and are called according to his purpose! It is his desire that you be in health, and prosper even as your soul prospers.

Some Heart Types in the Bible

God Prefers: Spirit-Led (Positive) 26

Grieved Heart	Genesis 6:6	Pure Heart	Psalm 24:4
Willing Heart	Exodus 25:2	Broken Heart	Psalm 34:18
Stirred Heart	Exodus 35:35	Panting Heart	Psalm 38:10
Another Heart	I Samuel 10:9	Failing Heart	Psalm 40:12
Perfect Heart	I Chronicles 12:38	Proclaiming Heart	Psalm 45:1
Tender Heart	II Chronicles 34:27	Established Fixed Heart	Psalm 57:7
Sorrowful Heart	Nehemiah 2:2-12	Living Heart	Psalm 69:32
Faithful Heart	Nehemiah 9:8	Established Heart	Psalm 112:8
Soft Heart	Job 23:16	Understanding Heart	Proverbs 2:2
Upright Heart	Job 33:3	Retaining Heart	Proverbs 4:4,21
Communing Heart	Psalm 4:4	Sound Heart	Proverbs 14:30
Heart of Wax	Psalm 22:14	Merry Heart	Proverbs 17:22
Wise Heart	Exodus 35:35	New Heart	Ezekiel 18:31 36:26

Some Heart Types in the Bible cont'd

God Despises: Flesh-Led (Negative) 25

Evil Heart	Genesis 6:5	Fat Greasy Heart	Psalm 119:70
Hardened Heart	Exodus 4:21	Desolate Heart	Psalm 143:4
Deceived Heart	Deuteronomy 11:16	Despising Heart	Proverbs 5:12
Non-Perceiving Heart	Deuteronomy 29:4	Deceitful Heart	Proverbs 12:20
Proud Heart	Psalm 101:5	Bitter Heart	Proverbs 14:10
Presumptuous Heart	Esther 7:5	Backslidden Heart	Proverbs 14:14
Hypocritical Heart	Job 36:13	Foolish Heart	Proverbs 15:7
Lifted-up Heart	Deuteronomy 8:14	Human Heart	Proverbs 15:11
Firm, Hard Heart	Job 41:24	Abominable Heart	Proverbs 26:25
Iniquitous Heart	Psalm 41:6	Double Heart	James 1:8
Wicked Heart	Psalm 58:2	Wounded Heart	Psalm 109:22
Erring Heart	Psalm 95:10	Evil Heart	Matthew 15:19
		Rebellious Heart	Jeremiah 5:23

Endnotes

MATERIALS
Bibles: King James Version

Books:
Myles Munroe, copyright 1991
Single, Married, Separated & Life After Divorce
Bahamas Faith Ministries Published by Vincom, Inc.
P.O. Box 702400
Tulsa, OK 74170
Reprint Permission Granted by Vincom, Inc.

Eugenia Price
Woman to Woman, copyright 1959
Zondervan Books
Zondervan Publishing House
Grand Rapids, MI 49506
Used by Permission of Zondervan Publishing House

Derek and Ruth Prince
God Is A Matchmaker, 1986
Chosen Books a Division of Baker Book House
P.O. Box 6287
Grand Rapids, MI 49516-6287
Used by Permission of Baker Book House

Spiros Zodhiates
The Complete Word Study – New Testament
Chattanooga, TN 37422
AMG Publishers, 1991
6815 Shallowford Rd.
Box 22000
Reprint Permission Granted by AMG Publishers

Other Volumes in the One Heart Series

VOLUME 1
With Oneness of Heart
ISBN 0-9700976-0-3
Formats: Paper, Audio, E-Book & Digital, Kindle
 Book: Disciple's Guide
Audio: Disciple's Overview

VOLUME 2
Book: Journeying to the Road Called Oneness
ISBN 0-9700976-1-1
Formats: Paper, Audio, E-Book & Digital, Kindle
 Book: Disciple's Guide
Audio: Disciple's Overview

VOLUME 3
Detouring off the Road of Oneness
ISBN 0-9700976-2-X
Formats: Paper, Audio, E-Book & Digital, Kindle
Book: Disciple's Guide
Audio: Disciple's Overview

VOLUME 4
I and My Father Are One
ISBN 0-9700976-3-8
Formats: Paper, Audio, E-Book & Digital, Kindle
Book: Disciple's Guide
Audio: Disciple's Overview

VOLUME 5
One Heart Series Devotional: 52 Week Study & Application
ISBN 09700976-7-0
Formats: Paperback

Website: www.oneheartseries.com
Affiliate Program: www.oneheartseriesaffiliates.com
Radio Network: www.oneheartsoundmedianetwork.com
Email: author@oneheartseries.com

www.ingramcontent.com/pod-product-compliance
Lightning Source LLC
Chambersburg PA
CBHW051623230426
43669CB00013B/2161